ON LIFE

ON LIFE

Philosophical Dialogues

Nicholas J. Pappas

Algora Publishing
New York

Library of Congress Cataloging-in-Publication Data —

Pappas, Nicholas J.
On life: philosophical dialogues / Nicholas J. Pappas.
    pages cm
  ISBN 978-1-62894-132-6 (soft cover: alk. paper) —ISBN 978-1-62894-133-3
(hard cover: alk. paper) —ISBN 978-1-62894-134-0 (ebook) 1. Life. 2. Conduct of life.
3. Imaginary conversations. I. Title.
  BD431 .P176 2015
  128—dc23
                            2014048262

Printed in the United States

TABLE OF CONTENTS

INTRODUCTION

What is this book and what is it not?

This book is an interwoven collection of short philosophical dialogues between four characters, where certain themes are taken up repeatedly, each time in a new light. This book is not a treatise. Who wants to read a strict treatise on life? I know I don't want to write one.

But what makes up this book? The interaction between the characters, what they say to one another. And by what they say to one another, I mean what they say to Director and what he says to them.

Director appears in all of the dialogues. He is the only character who does. In fact, the other characters — Friend, Artist, and Scientist — appear only one at a time. So we can say the book is nothing more than Director's conversations with them.

Who is Director? In some ways he resembles Socrates. But only in some ways. Director is our contemporary. He deals with issues other than those of Athens. Some of these issues grew out of ancient Greece. Many did not.

But Director differs from Plato's Socrates in another important way. He gives no long speeches such as those we find in *The Republic*, for instance. The dialogues in this book are emphatically short. Director employs a different technique.

But to what end? What is the book about? I can only point to the title and say — life!

Yes, but what can you say about life that hasn't already been said?

Maybe nothing. But if we weren't listening the last time through, it might be worth saying again.

So do I concede I say nothing new, that I just repeat the lessons of the past? Well, no. I freely admit I have no new doctrine to propound. But if I screw up my courage enough, I'm just bold enough to say — I offer a new approach.

Nick Pappas

1. Love 1 (Friend)

Director: What is love?

Friend: Love? It's just... love!

Director: It's just something you somehow know?

Friend: Yes.

Director: Can you try to describe how you somehow know it?

Friend: You know it because you feel it.

Director: Is that how we know things? We feel them?

Friend: That's how we know things like this.

Director: And what other things are things like this?

Friend: Hate, for one, I suppose.

Director: So we know what hate is through feeling it?

Friend: Yes.

Director: And that means if we never feel hate we can't really know what it is?

Friend: Right.

Director: The same holds for love?

Friend: Sure. If you've never loved, you don't know what love is.

Director: Now, when you hate, can the feeling go away?

Friend: Yes, but it's difficult to make it go away.

Director: And what about love? Can it go away?

Friend: Well, there's love and then there's love.

Director: I don't understand. Love isn't love?

Friend: There's more than one type of love.

Director: The kind that lasts and the kind that doesn't?

Friend: Exactly.

Director: Do these types of love feel different? Or do they feel the same and the only difference is in how long they last?

Friend: They feel different.

Director: Can you describe how they feel?

Friend: The love that lasts has friendship mixed into it.

Director: What does friendship feel like?

Friend: It just feels like... friendship.

Director: Then we'll assume we know what both love and friendship feel like. And that means we'll know when a love will last, right? We'll feel it. But then why would we ever waste our time on love that we know won't last?

Friend: We waste our time because we haven't learned our lesson yet.

Director: The lesson that we need friendship in our love?

Friend: Yes.

Director: I see. But now I'm wondering something about the love that doesn't last.

Friend: What are you wondering?

Director: I'm wondering whether it's possible. I mean, would you ever really feel love for someone who's not your friend? In other words, would you feel love for an enemy? Or for someone you're simply neutral toward? Those are all the possibilities, right? friend, neutral, enemy?

Friend: Well, we haven't talked about the difference between seeming friendship and true friendship.

Director: True love only comes with true friendship?

Friend: Right.

Director: But what is it you feel when there's no true friendship?

Friend: I don't know. I guess it must be some sort of confusion, a weird confusion.

Director: Do you think true friendship can develop from this confusion?

Friend: I think it's unlikely.

Director: Then if we feel a weird confusion, it seems there's little hope of love.

2. Happiness 1 (Artist)

Director: You know, Artist, I had an interesting conversation with Friend the other day.

Artist: Oh? About what?

Director: Love.

Artist: What did the two of you say?

Director: We said that true love involves friendship.

Artist: That's nice.

Director: And we said that when there's no friendship, and you feel a weird sort of confusion, you might think it's love, but it's not.

Artist: Ah, but Director, that weird sort of confusion is exactly what love is.

Director: Even when there's no friendship in the love?

Artist: Friendship concerns ordinary happiness.

Director: What's wrong with ordinary happiness?

Artist: Aside from being ordinary? It doesn't allow for greatness.

Director: And love without friendship does?

Artist: Haven't you noticed that all of the great loves are tempestuous? Why do you think that is?

Director: Because confusion reigns supreme?

Artist: Yes. And here's the thing. That confusion is intimately linked to creativity. It opens the mind to new ways.

Director: And having your mind opened to new ways takes you beyond ordinary happiness?

Artist: Yes. It takes you to great happiness. Sure, that doesn't mean you're happy all the time. How can it when you're tossed in the storm? But when you've managed to create, and there's a brief calm, you'll feel a happiness you wouldn't trade for anything in the whole world.

Director: In your view, is there any point to the confusion that we're calling love if it doesn't drive you to create?

Artist: No.

Director: But ordinary people can feel this confusion?

Artist: Yes. They just don't know what to do with it.

Director: But artists, in the broadest sense, do?

Artist: That's what makes an artist an artist.

Director: Does the artist need the stimulation of an ongoing confusion, or can confusion from the past be enough?

Artist: It's better if it's ongoing. There's more stimulation that way.

Director: But might there not be at times too much stimulation? Too great a storm?

Artist: Yes, I have to admit that's true.

Director: And won't this depend on how sensitive the artist is? I mean, if he's not very sensitive, he can weather great confusion. But if he's very sensitive, he can only handle small amounts. Or doesn't that seem how it is?

Artist: No, I guess that's how it is.

Director: What's better, to be a sensitive artist or an insensitive artist?

Artist: To be a sensitive artist.

Director: And if you're a sensitive artist, an extremely sensitive artist, and if what you've said about creativity and happiness is true — then is it possible that one memory of the sort of confusion we're talking about might be enough to sustain you, sustain you to the point of greatness? Or do you think an artist who's that sensitive really n

eeds ongoing confusion?

Artist: I suppose it's possible that one memory would suffice.

Director: Then if I were you I wouldn't go looking for any more trouble. Because you, Artist, are about as sensitive as they come. And if there's anything to what we've said, then it seems to me you have nothing to gain by being tossed once more in the storm.

3. TRUTH 1 (SCIENTIST)

Director: Scientist, I wonder if you can help me.

Scientist: How, Director?

Director: Do you believe we can know the truth about all things, or are there things we simply can never know the truth about?

Scientist: Maybe you can give me an example?

Director: I can give you two — love and happiness.

Scientist: The truth about these things is hard to know.

Director: But do you know the truth about them?

Scientist: No, I don't claim to know these things.

Director: But you know that it's possible to know the truth about them? How?

Scientist: You're right to ask. I don't know that it's possible to know the truth about them. But I believe it's possible.

Director: Because that's the faith of the scientist? Belief that it's possible to know all things?

Scientist: Yes.

Director: When you seek to know something how do you proceed?

Scientist: I devise experiments.

Director: So we would have to experiment with love and happiness in order to know about them?

Scientist: Yes, I suppose that's so.

Director: How would this experimenting be any different from the everyday gaining of experience that teaches all of us something about love and happiness?

Scientist: It would be different because it's controlled.

Director: Experience isn't controlled?

Scientist: Not generally. For the most part it's haphazard.

Director: But some people gain experience in a controlled manner? They're deliberate as they seek to learn?

Scientist: Yes. They proceed like scientists in their own lives. And they learn more than those who proceed haphazardly.

Director: Now here's something I'm wondering. If one of these people proceeds like a scientist and learns, comes to know what love and happiness are, can he do what scientists do concerning other things?

Scientist: What do you mean?

Director: I mean, can he publish his findings in a scientific journal?

Scientist: Of course not.

Director: Why not?

Scientist: Because he'd need to provide empirical data and demonstrate adherence to strict method in the collection of that data.

Director: In other words, we can't just take him on his word even if he's persuasive?

Scientist: Right. We need some scientific rigor and not just subjective certainty.

Director: And part of this rigor involves providing not just some but all of the details of his life experience as concerns love and happiness?

Scientist: Yes.

Director: In other words, he'd have to bare his soul completely?

Scientist: Precisely.

Director: Then instead of writing something for a scientific journal do you think he might be better served by writing an autobiography?

Scientist: I think that's an excellent idea.

Director: But do you think there can ever be what we might call a scientific autobiography?

Scientist: Loosely speaking? I'm inclined to think it's possible. But I'm aware of just how difficult something like that would be.

4. Lies 1 (Friend)

Director: What do you think is the worst kind of lie?

Friend: The worst kind? That's easy. It's the lie you tell yourself.

Director: If you tell yourself lies, does that mean you can't be objective when it comes to yourself?

Friend: Of course it does.

Director: So if you were to write an autobiography it wouldn't be objective either?

Friend: Certainly not.

Director: And an autobiography that's not objective wouldn't be of much use?

Friend: Well, it might be entertaining.

Director: But beyond entertainment?

Friend: I suppose you can learn about the author.

Director: How?

Friend: By studying what he says about himself.

Director: In order to figure out when he tells himself the truth?

Friend: Right, and when he tells himself a lie.

Director: But how would we be able to figure that out? I mean, won't he be the one presenting all the facts?

Friend: Sure, but he'll be giving his interpretation of the facts.

Director: And it's in the interpretation that we'll find the lie?

Friend: Exactly.

Director: But what if he lies about the facts?

Friend: Well, there's not much we can do about that.

Director: Unless we do some independent fact checking?

Friend: True, we could check the facts he presents. But it will be all but impossible to chase all the facts down. I mean, what if he says that when he was ten years old, he saved a boy from drowning?

Director: We find the boy, now man, and ask him to confirm.

Friend: And if this man says, no, you've got it wrong — I saved him?

Director: If there were no other witnesses, then I guess we're stuck.

Friend: And an averted drowning is a big fact. Imagine how many little facts in a person's life it's possible to lie about.

Director: I can imagine.

Friend: And that's not even to talk about all the untruths.

Director: You mean things he thinks he's telling the truth about but he's not?

Friend: Yes. Think about it. If you're telling yourself lies and believing them, what will you make of the facts in your life? Will you fix them in your mind according to a true standard or according to your lies?

Director: According to your lies.

Friend: Well, what you make of the facts determines how you remember them. And how you remember them determines how you'll write about them, at least when you're trying to be honest.

Director: So is there really much point to reading something by someone who lies to himself?

Friend: No, I don't think there is. Once you get the sense someone is a liar it's best to leave him and his work well enough alone.

Director: But, if we get that sense, couldn't we let him know we see he's telling lies? Might that not encourage him to stop?

Friend: Stop? The liars I know, when confronted, tell even greater lies.

Director: Then maybe we can find another way to approach these liars, a way other than direct confrontation — a way that leaves an out, a way of saving face?

Friend: In hopes that they'll then start telling the truth? I'm sorry to say it, Director, but that strikes me as more than just a little naive.

5. Lies 2 (*Artist*)

Artist: I aim for an honesty in my work.

Director: And you believe people pick up on this honesty?

Artist: Of course.

Director: All people or just certain people?

Artist: Those who are honest with themselves.

Director: So someone who lies to himself can't pick up on when you're being honest?

Artist: I think it's unlikely. Someone like that sees the world through a distorted lens.

Director: And to appreciate the honesty of your work you need a lens that's true?

Artist: Yes. After all, what do those who lie to themselves care about truth?

Director: Oh, I think they care a great deal about truth. They care about hiding it. No?

Artist: Well, my aim is the opposite of that.

Director: Then tell me. In the works of yours I've seen, you always seem to depict the beautiful right alongside the ugly. Is that intentional?

Artist: Of course it is.

Director: Why do you put them together?

Artist: Because I want to bring out all of the truth — the beautiful and ugly alike.

Director: And the people who take in your work, what do they prefer — the beautiful or the ugly?

Artist: Most appreciate the beautiful, a few appreciate the ugly, and some appreciate both.

Director: Which of these sorts of people do you like best?

Artist: Those who appreciate both the beautiful and the ugly.

Director: Because they appreciate all of your work, all of your truth, and not just part of it?

Artist: Yes.

Director: And those who only appreciate part of it, if they could, do you think they would try to hide the part that they don't like?

Artist: You mean those who only appreciate the beautiful would hide the ugly, and those who only appreciate the ugly would hide the beautiful?

Director: Yes. And if they were to do so, wouldn't they be hiding part of the truth?

Artist: Well, yes.

Director: But since they can't have their way with your work like that, what do they do?

Artist: They turn a blind eye to the parts of it they don't like.

Director: So someone who only appreciates the beautiful will turn a blind eye to the ugly, and someone who only appreciates the ugly will turn a blind eye to the beautiful?

Artist: Yes.

Director: And in this blind eye don't you think we find a sort of lie?

Artist: I suppose we can say that — a lie to oneself, a lie that the ugly or the beautiful isn't there.

Director: But the ugly and the beautiful is always there?

Artist: It is. Beauty can't exist without a corresponding ugliness in the world, just as ugliness can't exist without a corresponding beauty.

Director: Sort of like there can be no good without a corresponding evil and no evil without a corresponding good?

Artist: Just so.

Director: Well, Artist, if that's what you believe, then I can see you're honest in your work.

Artist: Thank you, Director.

Director: But I have a question. Doesn't the beautiful seek to separate itself from the ugly at times?

Artist: Yes, but the ugly doesn't want to let it go.

Director: Then maybe you can try to depict a fleeing beauty instead of one that merely sits alongside ugliness?

Artist: Yes, I think that's a good idea. But then once I've done that I'm going to depict beauty attempting to drive ugliness out.

Director: But ugliness will always return?

Artist: Yes, if what I believe is true.

Director: And if it isn't?

Artist: Then I'll admit I was wrong. And I'll learn to show the two all on their own.

6. LIES 3 (*SCIENTIST*)

Director: Does science recognize the difference between beauty and ugliness?

Scientist: Well, we can say the healthy and successful is the beautiful.

Director: And the sickly and unsuccessful is the ugly?

Scientist: Yes, from the perspective of science. But there are other perspectives.

Director: There certainly are. But tell me. What if one of the sickly, in hopes of becoming beautiful, disguises itself as one of the healthy?

Scientist: Are we talking about animals or humans?

Director: Does it matter?

Scientist: Of course it does.

Director: Why?

Scientist: Because animals can't tell lies.

Director: But can't they try to disguise themselves?

Scientist: Sure, but they can't make up stories about themselves the way humans can — at least that we're aware of.

Director: So let's say we're talking about humans. Can science tell if someone is lying about himself, claiming to be healthy when really he's sick?

Scientist: If it has the chance to examine this person? Yes, almost certainly.

Director: But what about when it comes to success? Can science tell if someone who's unsuccessful is disguising himself as one of the successful?

Scientist: Well, I don't know about that. There are so many subjective factors involved.

Director: So science can't tell if a human is lying about how successful he is? It can't tell that he's merely saying he's very happy when in actual fact he's not?

Scientist: I think it would be hard to know that with certainty.

Director: Why would someone say he's happy when he's not? Would it be in order to appear beautiful?

Scientist: That sounds a little odd, but yes, I think it's true.

Director: Now I'm wondering about something. Would you say that part of appearing beautiful is having a good self-image?

Scientist: I would say that part of being beautiful, and not merely appearing so, is having one.

Director: So if you lie about having a good self-image, you might appear beautiful but not actually be beautiful?

Scientist: Yes, I suppose.

Director: But can you lie your way into actually having a good self-image?

Scientist: That's an interesting question. I don't know. I mean, on the one hand, if you know your self-image is based on lies, I don't see how you can feel good about it. But on the other hand, if you believe your lies, then maybe it's possible to actually have a good self-image.

Director: And a good self-image is always beautiful?

Scientist: Well, I don't like to say that.

Director: You'd rather say that a good self-image based on truth is always beautiful?

Scientist: Yes.

Director: But what if the truth is ugly?

Scientist: You can't have a truly good self-image if your truth is ugly.

Director: So what can you do in that case?

Scientist: You have to find a way to change your truth, to make it beautiful — which is very much easier said than done.

7. Birth (Artist)

Director: Have you ever heard it said that artists give birth to their works?

Artist: Yes, I have.

Director: Why do you think people say this?

Artist: Because works of art grow within an artist over time, are difficult to deliver, and lead a life of their own once they're born.

Director: Yes, but unlike actual births, artistic births can be controlled to some extent, right?

Artist: In what sense?

Director: In the sense that an artist can control whether he gives birth to a truth or a lie. Or don't you think an artist has that control?

Artist: No, I think he does.

Director: Now, when an artist gives birth to a truth, would you say that truth is beautiful?

Artist: Of course.

Director: And when an artist gives birth to a lie?

Artist: I'd say that lie is ugly.

Director: Are truths always beautiful?

Artist: Well, we sometimes speak of the ugly truth.

Director: And do we sometimes speak of a beautiful lie?

Artist: Sometimes.

Director: I have a pretty good sense of what an ugly truth is. But what's a beautiful lie?

Artist: It's something that isn't true but that people really want to hear.

Director: Are you satisfied when you encounter something that isn't true that you want to hear?

Artist: Me? No, I'm only satisfied with the truth itself — beautiful, ugly, or something in-between.

Director: So lies aren't beautiful to you?

Artist: Of course they're not.

Director: But they're beautiful to others?

Artist: Yes.

Director: So in a popularity contest it's possible that a beautiful lie will win out over an ugly truth?

Artist: I'd say it's more than possible. It's likely.

Director: And what happens if an ugly lie goes up against a beautiful truth?

Artist: The beautiful truth will almost certainly win.

Director: And in a competition between a beautiful lie and a beautiful truth?

Artist: That's not so easy to decide.

Director: Because by beautiful we mean something that people want to hear, and in this case people want to hear both the truth and the lie?

Artist: Right.

Director: Would it matter to them if they knew that the truth took years and years of gestation, and involved a birth of almost unbelievable difficulty, and then required many years of careful nurturing before it was ready to stand on its own? And would it matter to them if they knew that the gestation of the lie was the matter of a night, and that the birth was so easy that no one even noticed the lie was born, and that the lie sprang at once from the womb to its feet?

Artist: Director, I know what you're saying. But I think what you've said would be an argument for many in favor of the lie.

Director: But why?

Artist: Who wants to think about all that effort and pain?

Director: Do you?

Artist: In what you said you described my own experience and work. But I have to tell you the truth. I don't like to think about all that I went through to bring my truths to light. So why should I expect that anyone else would?

Director: Then how do we ensure that the beautiful truth wins out against the beautiful lie?

Artist: There's only one way. We make it look easy.

8. Control (Scientist)

Scientist: So you're not talking about control in the strictly scientific sense?

Director: No, I mean control in the general sense.

Scientist: Well, let's start from common sense. People say they want to be in control of the situation, right?

Director: That's true. But what does it mean to be in control?

Scientist: You dictate what will happen.

Director: So if you're an artist, and you have a showing of your work, to be in control would mean to dictate how people react to your work?

Scientist: Well, some situations allow for control and some don't.

Director: But can't an artist control what his work is?

Scientist: Yes, but he can't control how people will react to it.

Director: But what if he knows the people? What if he gears his work precisely to those people?

Scientist: But then he's not controlling how they'll react. He's reacting to how they'll react.

Director: So the audience controls the artist?

Scientist: Yes, if the artist wants to get a certain reaction out of the audience.

Director: Then those artists who think they can control their audience are deluded?

Scientist: In the worst way.

Director: What's the scientific term for such delusion?

Scientist: I'd say it's confusing the cause.

Director: The cause is the way the people are?

Scientist: Yes.

Director: But the artist thinks the cause is his work?

Scientist: Right.

Director: But doesn't the work cause the reaction in the audience? I mean, without the work there would be no reaction.

Scientist: True, just as without the audience there would be no reaction.

Director: So what are we saying? Isn't the cause really the bringing together of the audience and the work?

Scientist: That sounds better.

Director: But then who's really in control here?

Scientist: I guess it's the one who brings the audience and the work together.

Director: You mean someone like the promoter or the gallery owner?

Scientist: Sure. Think of it like chemistry. The one in control is the one who brings the substances together for a reaction.

Director: If you were an artist, would it matter who brings you together with your audience? Isn't the fact of their reaction enough? Or is that too cynical a view?

Scientist: No, I don't think it's cynical. I think it's true. It wouldn't matter who brought you together with your audience.

Director: And what about the audience? Would it matter to them who brought them to their artist?

Scientist: No, it's the same as with the artist. All they care about is their reaction.

Director: Then the one in control doesn't matter to either artist or audience?

Scientist: Well, it matters whether the one in control brings about good or bad reactions.

Director: And that would depend on how well he knows both artist and audience?

Scientist: Of course.

Director: But if the artist and the audience knew both themselves and each other, couldn't they do without someone to bring them together? Couldn't they do it themselves?

Scientist: They could. But what you're talking about is rare.

Director: Because knowledge of the other is rare?

Scientist: Because knowledge of yourself is rare.

9. Freedom 1 (*Artist*)

Artist: Freedom is all about being free from control.

Director: Would you include self-control in that statement?

Artist: Self-control? No, of course not.

Director: So it's only control from others that we want to be free of?

Artist: Yes.

Director: And how do others control us?

Artist: They tell us what to do or not to do.

Director: And when they tell us what to do or not to do, do they always do so directly?

Artist: What do you mean?

Director: I mean, couldn't they employ subtle pressures and suggestions?

Artist: Sure, but that doesn't mean they control us.

Director: Is that so even if you're someone that's susceptible to subtle pressures and suggestions?

Artist: You mean if you're weak?

Director: Well, yes.

Artist: If you're weak, you're easily controlled.

Director: Yes, I think that's true. But now I regret what I said.

Artist: Why?

Director: Because I didn't distinguish between being susceptible to subtle pressures and suggestions and being sensitive to them. The former might mean you're weak, but does the latter? Aren't artists supposed to be very sensitive? Does that make them weak?

Artist: Of course not.

Director: So if you're sensitive to subtle pressures and so on, how do you deal with them so that you're not manipulated?

Artist: You have to learn to ignore them.

Director: Is ignoring them a sort of self-control? I mean, you control yourself and ignore before you allow yourself to be controlled?

Artist: Yes, that's right.

Director: Would you say you have to be strong to exercise self-control?

Artist: I would.

Director: When would you exercise the most self-control and therefore be most strong? When you have only a few subtle pressures and suggestions to deal with or when you're completely surrounded?

Artist: When you're surrounded.

Director: I'm inclined to agree. But tell me. If you're always ignoring these things, how do you differ from someone who's simply insensitive and doesn't notice them at all?

Artist: Well, you don't ignore them all. Sometimes you pay close attention.

Director: Why?

Artist: Because pressures and suggestions are sometimes the preliminaries to more aggressive behavior.

Director: Behavior that would take away your freedom?

Artist: Yes. That's why you have to know enough to not just ignore but to deal with such behavior in its earliest form, to nip it in the bud.

Director: But what if there's always bad behavior to nip?

Artist: Then that's just the price of being free.

10. Freedom 2 (Friend)

Friend: But don't we give our attention to more than just those whom we suspect might become aggressive?

Director: Who do you have in mind?

Friend: Anyone who isn't trying to manipulate us.

Director: But if they're not trying to manipulate us, why do you think they bother with all the pressures and suggestions?

Friend: Maybe that's where we're wrong.

Director: What do you mean?

Friend: Maybe the people we're talking about now, the ones who aren't interested in manipulating us — maybe they don't employ any sort of pressures or suggestions.

Director: What do they employ?

Friend: Hints.

Director: And what are these hints about?

Friend: They might be about the nature of the person dropping the hints.

Director: If the person's nature is any good, then why does he have to deal in hints?

Friend: It might be because he's looking for freedom.

Director: Freedom? How?

Friend: Do you believe you need recognition in order to be free?

Director: Recognition for what you are?

Friend: Yes.

Director: We can say that recognition is an element of freedom.

Friend: Well, what if the only way this person knows how to be recognized is through hints?

Director: I don't know, Friend. I'm not so sure that's a good way to go.

Friend: You mean you don't believe in dropping hints about yourself?

Director: No, I don't.

Friend: So you wouldn't pay attention to those who do?

Director: No, I would.

Friend: Why?

Director: Because I'd like to persuade them of something.

Friend: What?

Director: To forget about hints and speak clearly about themselves. That's the way to the freedom we're talking about, as far as I can tell. But, you know, I have a doubt. I'm not sure people use hints merely because that's the only way they know how to be recognized.

Friend: Why do they use hints then?

Director: Because they're afraid.

Friend: Afraid of what?

Director: The very thing they think they want — the freedom that comes from recognition.

Friend: Yes, but now I have a doubt. Are they afraid of the freedom, or are they afraid of the recognition?

Director: In the end, I don't know that it makes much difference, Friend.

11. Memory (*Friend*)

Friend: If you learn something about someone, do you think you'd ever forget?

Director: You mean like the person's name?

Friend: No, of course not. People forget names all the time. I mean something important.

Director: What's important?

Friend: Something about the way the person is.

Director: You mean something essential?

Friend: Yes.

Director: It seems unlikely you'd forget something essential.

Friend: Well, suppose you're focused on learning essential things. Do you think you'd have a tendency to forget the non-essential?

Director: I'm not sure. But maybe it will help if you give me an example of something essential and something non-essential?

Friend: We've already mentioned something that's non-essential — a person's name.

Director: Do you think that names are non-essential only when it comes to people, or do you think names are non-essential when it comes to things, too?

Friend: I think they're non-essential for things, as well.

Director: So if you go into a store and say you want to buy one of those hard and sparkly rocks, they'll know what you mean without your saying you want a diamond?

Friend: Yes, exactly.

Director: What's the essential in this example?

Friend: The hardness and the sparkle.

Director: And by remembering the essential you've remembered enough?

Friend: Yes.

Director: Now if you do this once or twice, I assume people won't think anything of it. But what happens if you do this all the time?

Friend: People will think there's something wrong with you.

Director: Even though you remember the essential?

Friend: Even though.

Director: So we remember the non-essential in order not to have people think something is wrong with us?

Friend: Well, that's not the only reason.

Director: What other reason is there?

Friend: It isn't always good to say the essential. I mean, what if the essential is negative? For instance, is it good to say you're talking about the ugly boy who lies a lot? It might be better if you just say the boy's name.

Director: Because names are neutral?

Friend: Right.

Director: And they're neutral because they allow us to conceal what we really think, good or bad?

Friend: Yes.

Director: And it's important at times to conceal what we think? Essential, even?

Friend: I think that's true.

Director: Then why would we ever forget a name?

12. MEMORIES (*ARTIST*)

Artist: I can't believe you didn't talk about the ease of communication that comes with names. Can you imagine if everyone had to spell out all of the essentials for each thing all the time? You know, that wet stuff that comes in drops and falls from the sky? It would be a madhouse.

Director: Yes, you're making a good point. I'll have to take this up with Friend again. But what do you think about the rest of our conversation?

Artist: I'm hung up on what you said about the importance of the neutral.

Director: Oh? Why?

Artist: It has to do with how I think our memories work.

Director: You don't think we have neutral memories?

Artist: No, I think we do. But we also have good memories and bad memories — and we're far more likely to remember the good and the bad than the neutral.

Director: So if someone wants to make an impression on us, it's best to be either very good or very bad?

Artist: Right, and then we're likely to remember.

Director: This means that our memories are filled with the names of the good and the bad?

Artist: Yes.

Director: While the neutrals are lost to oblivion?

Artist: I'm afraid that's the truth of it.

Director: Well, let me ask you this. Is it really only the very good and the very bad we remember? Or do we also remember, for example, those who are very skilled and those who aren't very skilled?

Artist: I think we remember the ones who are very skilled and not the ones who aren't.

Director: Why not the ones who aren't? What if they're bad at whatever skill we're talking about?

Artist: Yes, but the kind of bad I was talking about has more to do with moral things than skill.

Director: Then we remember both the morally good, the morally bad, and the skilled — and that's it? But what about someone who is, for instance, an absolutely terrible pianist? Are you sure we won't remember him?

Artist: Well, if he's terrible, and I mean really terrible, we might remember.

Director: We'd remember because his performance is ridiculous?

Artist: Yes.

Director: What's the opposite of the ridiculous?

Artist: The awe inspiring.

Director: So we're likely to remember both the things that fill us with laughter and the things that fill us with awe?

Artist: Yes, we are.

Director: But do bad and good reduce to laughter and awe?

Artist: Of course not.

Director: Because the bad isn't always funny and the good isn't always awe inspiring?

Artist: Right.

Director: Alright. Now, if you don't mind, I'd like to consider an example.

Artist: By all means.

Director: Suppose there's a great dispute, and both sides are making arguments for their case, and making them very well. Might we remember the people who make the case for either side?

Artist: If it's a truly great dispute? Yes.

Director: But what if, though both sides are making spectacular arguments, you can see that both sides are actually in the wrong? Would you still remember them?

Artist: I would, because they're spectacularly wrong.

Director: Now what if someone stands up in the middle, a lone neutral, and simply says both sides are wrong and gives the basic reasons why, but gives them with neither too much nor too little skill?

Artist: He makes just an average sort of presentation? Just a simple statement of the reasons why?

Director: Yes. Would you remember this person?

Artist: Of course I would.

Director: Why? Isn't he just a forgettable neutral, lost in the larger debate?

Artist: No, he's far from that. He's someone who speaks truth. And you can never be a mere neutral when you speak truth.

13. PETS 1 (FRIEND)

Director: What's the difference between a human and a pet?

Friend: Are you being serious?

Director: Yes.

Friend: Why do you want to know?

Director: Because I want to know the truth about humans. And humans often have pets.

Friend: Then why bother with the difference between humans and their pets? Why not just focus on what the pets give their humans?

Director: What do they give them?

Friend: Love.

Director: How do humans know their pets love them?

Friend: Because their pets show affection.

Director: Just like humans show affection?

Friend: Yes, but affection from pets is more pure.

Director: More pure? What do you mean?

Friend: I just mean that people are more complicated than pets.

Director: And just because something is complicated it means it can't be as pure?

Friend: Well, no, not exactly. But it's more difficult to get through to the purity. That's what I really meant to say.

Director: Why is it more difficult?

Friend: Because life gets in the way.

Director: I've often heard that phrase but I've never understood what it means.

Friend: It's not so difficult to understand. It just means that life is complicated.

Director: But it's not complicated for pets?

Friend: No, it's generally not.

Director: And so it's easier for them to get through to the purity of affection?

Friend: Yes.

Director: And if easier, then their affection is generally more reliable?

Friend: Yes, you can always count on a loving pet.

Director: Now, humans, they don't always get through to the purity of affection?

Friend: They rarely do.

Director: And what happens when they don't?

Friend: You can't always count on them.

Director: I see. Well, it seems we wound up answering my question.

Friend: You mean the difference between humans and their pets?

Director: Yes. We seem to be saying they're essentially the same, at least when it comes to love — except life tends to get in the way for humans and it doesn't for pets.

Friend: But don't you think people will think we're crazy if they hear us saying that humans and their pets are essentially the same concerning something as important as love?

Director: If what we're saying is true, then why should we care?

14. Method 1 (Scientist)

Scientist: Do I believe that the love of an animal is the same as that of a human? I'm not sure. I'd have to prove it one way or the other. But I'd start with the love of humans.

Director: Why?

Scientist: Because we can ask humans what love means to them. We can't ask animals.

Director: But what if you get all sorts of different and even contradictory answers?

Scientist: Then we'll simply have to observe human behavior and decide on our own what behavior constitutes love.

Director: But how will we know if something is love?

Scientist: We can form hypotheses about what love is and then test those hypotheses.

Director: So one of those hypotheses might, for instance, be that love involves loyalty?

Scientist: Sure.

Director: And if we see humans exhibiting this type of loyalty we can conclude that these humans love?

Scientist: No, it doesn't work that way. It might be possible to show loyalty without love. But let's try this. Have you felt love?

Director: I have.

Scientist: How would you describe it?

Director: Now you're trying to embarrass me.

Scientist: Embarrass you? How?

Director: I think it's very difficult to describe love.

Scientist: Why don't you try?

Director: Alright. I'll say that love is a strong feeling of attraction.

Scientist: Ah, but that's romantic love. We want love in the broadest possible sense.

Director: So that it includes all types of love? But what if one type of love differs fundamentally from the others?

Scientist: Fundamentally? Then we need to make separate inquiries. We'll proceed methodically, one love at a time.

Director: Good. So there's romantic love, for one. What other types should we consider?

Scientist: Two types — love of family and love of friends.

Director: But aren't the loves of family and friends, essentially, the same type of love?

Scientist: We can assume that if you like.

Director: Yes, let's assume it. So we begin with two types of human love. We can get particular about how exactly we define them later, right? But now I see a problem.

Scientist: What problem?

Director: What if in addition to different types of love there are different types of humans, different types who experience each of these two types of love in different ways?

Scientist: You're asking whether love differs from human to human?

Director: Yes. How do we proceed then? What's our method?

Scientist: I suppose we have to seek to classify human beings according to how they experience the different types of love.

Director: And once we come up with our system of classification, is there any reason why we can't then see how it applies to animals?

Scientist: I see no reason why we couldn't try to classify animals as we classify humans. But then we might find that, in a way, certain animals and humans are more like one another than they're like their fellow animals and humans. And I'm not sure we're ready to believe that, even if we think it's true.

15. Madness 1 (Artist)

Artist: More alike than we thought? That may be. But I'll tell you how humans and animals differ. Animals don't go mad, at least not in the way that humans do.

Director: How do you know?

Artist: Because animals don't create art.

Director: And art is a sign of madness?

Artist: Of course.

Director: If art is a sign, what's the underlying cause?

Artist: Well, some people will tell you it's just a chemical thing. But I'll tell you what I think the real cause is. Love.

Director: Have you gone mad with love?

Artist: I have. I'm not ashamed to admit it.

Director: Is your love unrequited?

Artist: No, not exactly.

Director: Who do you love?

Artist: It isn't who, Director. It's what. I love life.

Director: But don't people love life all the time?

Artist: Yes, but I love life with an artist's intensity.

Director: And what's the nature of that intensity?

Artist: Here's the best way I know to sum it up. Sometimes life seems so beautiful that it hurts. And while you experience this beauty you can't help but think that one day it will be gone.

Director: So you try to capture that fleeting beauty?

Artist: Yes.

Director: That doesn't seem mad to me.

Artist: But the pain is so bad that it makes you crazy.

Director: But then you channel this craziness into your work, right?

Artist: Right.

Director: And does the craziness overflow the banks at times?

Artist: It does.

Director: What happens then?

Artist: I ruin my work.

Director: So you have to create at just the right moment, when you're crazy but not too crazy?

Artist: Yes.

Director: Wouldn't it be easier if you could regulate how crazy you get?

Artist: Of course it would. But how would I do that?

Director: Can you limit how much you love life?

Artist: But if I do that then I wouldn't be who I am.

Director: You mean you can't be an artist without as an intense love of life as you sometimes have, a love that floods your being with madness and ruins your work?

Artist: Well, maybe I would limit my love to the extent that it prevents a flood.

Director: And how would you do that?

Artist: I'm not sure. But something occurs to me, something that means I don't have to limit how much I love life.

Director: What?

Artist: I can dig my channels deeper.

Director: So you'd be able to handle more madness?

Artist: Yes. The deeper I go, the more intensely I can love.

Director: And if you go deeper, your work becomes more profound?

Artist: Of course.

Director: Well, Artist, that sounds fine. But just make sure of one thing. When you go deep, please take care that you don't drown.

16. Belief (*Scientist*)

Director: Scientist, do you believe what we believe is important?

Scientist: I know that what we believe is important.

Director: You know this as a scientist?

Scientist: I know this as a man.

Director: So you would say it matters, for instance, that Artist seems to believe that pain is a necessary ingredient to his art?

Scientist: Of course.

Director: Now, when we say belief matters, what exactly matters?

Scientist: Whether the belief is true or false.

Director: So if, again for example, Artist is right, and pain is indeed a necessary ingredient to his art, then his belief is true. But what follows from that?

Scientist: He knows he has to put up with the pain, if he wants to keep making art.

Director: But if he's wrong, and his belief is false?

Scientist: Then the pain is unnecessary.

Director: And he won't be free of the pain until he comes to see his belief is false?

Scientist: Yes.

Director: How can someone like Artist come to see his belief is false, if we can assume it is indeed false?

Scientist: He could try to create when he feels no pain.

Director: And if he can in fact create, then he knows he was wrong?

Scientist: Well, it's not that simple.

Director: Why not?

Scientist: Because what if he creates something, but it's not as good as what he creates when he's in pain?

Director: Who's to say how good it is? Artist?

Scientist: Yes, sure. Ultimately he's the one who has to believe his art is as good without pain as with it.

Director: But couldn't an objective judge try to persuade him that his art is just as good, assuming that what he creates is in fact just as good?

Scientist: Again, it's not so simple.

Director: Why?

Scientist: Because there's no such thing as a truly objective judge.

Director: What do you mean?

Scientist: We have to take into account what the judge believes.

Director: You mean the judge might believe that art from a tortured artist is better than art from one who isn't tortured?

Scientist: Yes, precisely. And if we pick a judge who believes that art from an artist who creates with no pain is best, we're just prejudiced the other way.

Director: Hmm. But can we really tell when art comes from a tortured artist or from one who feels no pain? In other words, is there something peculiar about the works of art created by someone in pain?

Scientist: Well, how would we know? You can fake both pain and the lack of pain, after all.

Director: But won't the faker come off as inauthentic?

Scientist: Not necessarily. There are some good fakers out there, Director.

Director: So it's best to judge simply by the work of art itself, and not by the state of the artist when he created it?

Scientist: Yes, I think that's best.

Director: Then we can't tell the judge what the state of the artist was during creation. We can only present the judge with the finished work.

Scientist: Agreed.

Director: And if the artist created without pain, and the judge thinks very highly of the work, and we repeat this test over and over again with different judges and get the same results — then wouldn't that give the artist confidence that he can create good work without pain?

Scientist: If it didn't, then I don't know what would. But beliefs are hard to change. Sometimes they can, as with an artist's belief in and dependence on pain, be used as a crutch. And letting go of a long held crutch is never an easy thing.

17. PREMISES (FRIEND)

Friend: Pain isn't always bad. You know the saying — no pain, no gain.

Director: So if someone operates from the premise that pain is good, you wouldn't think he's necessarily wrong?

Friend: It depends on what else he thinks. If he thinks that all that comes of the pain is pain, then no — I'd think he's wrong.

Director: But if he thinks something good comes from the pain?

Friend: And something good actually does come from the pain? Then I'd think it's okay to think that pain is good.

Director: But can't he think that pain is bad but brings something good?

Friend: Sure.

Director: Isn't that the better way to look at it? I mean, isn't pain in and of itself always bad?

Friend: Yes, I know what you mean. Pain, as pain, is always bad. Strictly speaking it doesn't make sense to say anything else.

Director: Then why do some people seem to start from the premise that pain, if it brings something good, is good?

Friend: You mean why do they persuade themselves of something that's not true?

Director: Yes.

Friend: Maybe it makes the pain easier to take.

Director: So if I'm starving, it would make starving easier to take if I think starving is good because it brings something good?

Friend: That's the logic of it. But I'm not sure it would make starving any easier to take.

Director: So why not tell it like it is? Starving is bad no matter what it brings.

Friend: I would. You would. But not everyone would.

Director: Why?

Friend: Ask an anorexic.

Director: What's the anorexic's fundamental premise?

Friend: That good comes of starving.

Director: And everyone but the anorexic knows that premise is false?

Friend: Yes.

Director: Is there any way to persuade the anorexic that the premise is false?

Friend: I think there is. But it's very difficult.

Director: Because the anorexic is sick?

Friend: Yes.

Director: Are those who operate on false premises always sick?

Friend: In a sense I think that's true.

Director: And to help them get better we have to bring them to true premises?

Friend: Yes. They need to operate on premises that will actually bring them good.

Director: What are the biggest challenges we'll face in trying to get them to adopt true premises?

Friend: Well, first we have to know what premises are true ourselves.

Director: And it's not always easy to know?

Friend: No, it's not.

Director: So what other challenges do we face?

Friend: In many cases we'll have to get the sick ones to break longstanding habits.

Director: And that's never easy, right? What else?

Friend: This one is a bit complicated, and is in my opinion the most difficult to deal with. Some people who act on false premises suffer much from those premises — and they can't bear to think that all their pain has been for nothing. So they want to keep on throwing good money after bad, as the saying goes. We have to teach them not to squander their remaining cash.

18. LOGIC (ARTIST)

Artist: The problem with logic is that it assumes some reasoning is valid and some reasoning is invalid.

Director: And to artists all reasoning is valid?

Artist: Yes.

Director: Can you give me an example of valid reasoning?

Artist: Sure. Pigs can fly; cats are pigs; therefore cats can fly. What do you think?

Director: Technically speaking? If I remember my definitions correctly, the argument is valid because it's such that it's impossible for the premises to be true and the conclusion to be false. But the argument is unsound because the premises aren't true.

Artist: Well, this is precisely the sort of argument that artists often use.

Director: Why?

Artist: Because the false presented in valid form has a certain power.

Director: What power?

Artist: A power operating on the imagination.

Director: This must be one of the mysteries of art that I've never understood.

Artist: It's not really a mystery. Artists stir the imagination with false premises and false conclusions all the time. They just have to make them seem plausible.

Director: How do they do that?

Artist: They present them as metaphors. And can you really say that metaphors are true or false? Don't you simply have to say whether they're compelling or not?

Director: So in your little argument, pigs and cats and flying all stand for something?

Artist: Of course.

Director: What if you put the things they stand for into the argument?

Artist: Then the argument is less interesting.

Director: Less interesting because artists want people to have to exercise their imagination, to make the leap from the metaphor to what the metaphor stands for?

Artist: Yes.

Director: And some people will make the right leap and some the wrong leap?

Artist: Not exactly. You see, for some artists there is no right or wrong leap.

Director: How can that be? I thought we said the metaphors stand for something.

Artist: Yes, but artists don't always know what their metaphors stand for.

Director: You mean the audience tells the artist what the art means?

Artist: For many artists I think that's true, though I don't know how many would admit it.

Director: And when is there greater need for the audience to tell the artist what it all means — when an artist uses valid or invalid arguments?

Artist: Let me give you an example of what logic calls an invalid argument; then see what you think. Pigs can fly; cats are pigs; therefore pigs love cats. Well?

Director: Well, I suppose the audience will wonder what pigs and cats stand for, as with the valid argument. And, again as with the valid argument, they might wonder about flying pigs, and what it means for cats to be pigs. But then they might also wonder why pigs love cats. And they might even wonder if cats return the love. So I guess this argument has more to wonder about, more room for leaping — and more need for the artist to hear what the audience thinks.

Artist: Why do you think an artist might prefer to use an argument like this?

Director: I suppose if all the artist cares about is making the audience leap somewhere, anywhere, an invalid argument might be best. But is this the sort of argument you employ, Artist?

Artist: At times. But I don't want the audience to leap just anywhere. I want it to leap to the truth.

Director: Then why make it leap at all? Why not walk it straight to the truth?

Artist: Because then it wouldn't be art.

19. Emotions (*Artist*)

Director: Do you feel all of the emotions you depict, Artist?

Artist: Do you mean at the time I depict them? Of course not.

Director: But at some time prior to depicting them?

Artist: Mostly.

Director: If only mostly, that means you can portray an emotion you've never felt?

Artist: I can.

Director: How do you do that?

Artist: I simply study someone who feels the emotion and report what I see.

Director: What's the ugliest emotion you've seen?

Artist: Hatred.

Director: Have you ever felt hatred?

Artist: True hatred? No.

Director: Have you shown that emotion in your art?

Artist: I have.

Director: So you've studied someone who felt hatred?

Artist: Yes.

Director: How did you go about doing that?

Artist: What do you mean?

Director: I mean did you introduce yourself and say I'd like to spend some time together while I study the emotion you feel?

Artist: Of course not.

Director: Then how did you go about studying it?

Artist: People in my life from time to time show hatred.

Director: But if no one in your life shows hatred? Do you have to seek someone out who does?

Artist: I suppose.

Director: What do you think is better? Finding an emotion among those who are already in your life, or going out and finding people with that emotion then bringing them into your life?

Artist: I'm not sure.

Director: Okay. But I'm surprised you didn't object.

Artist: To what?

Director: To the notion that you might have to bring certain people with certain emotions into your life.

Artist: If you really want to study someone, to know someone, you need to be engaged. And to be engaged you need that person in your life in one way or another.

Director: How many artists do you think voluntarily go out and engage with people who have very ugly emotions?

Artist: I don't know. I think that's a hard thing to do.

Director: It's easier if you already have people in your life who have these emotions?

Artist: I don't know about that.

Director: Why not?

Artist: Because it's hard to engage with these people regardless of where you find them.

Director: But if they're already in your life, aren't you forced to engage?

Artist: Not necessarily.

Director: What happens if you don't?

Artist: Besides not becoming an artist? You suffer from your ignorance.

Director: What's a sign that someone is suffering from his ignorance?

Artist: Believing that the ugly is other than what it is.

20. Revenge (Artist)

Director: What's the best revenge an artist can take?

Artist: Showing things as they are.

Director: So that the object of revenge will look bad and the artist will look good?

Artist: Not necessarily.

Director: You mean the object of revenge will look good and the artist will look bad?

Artist: Of course not. The object of revenge will look bad, but the artist doesn't have to look either good or bad.

Director: Ah, you mean the artist will appear neutral, objective?

Artist: Yes.

Director: And that makes the revenge all the more sweet? I mean, people will assume that because you're neutral you must be objective and therefore must be showing things as they really are?

Artist: That's right.

Director: But are you really neutral, or do you present your subject in... a certain light?

Artist: Well, artists are all about light, after all.

Director: But doesn't presenting things in a certain light amount to tipping the scales?

Artist: But that's how the world is. We all see things according to our own lights.

Director: And none of those lights are neutral or objective, not even the light of the sun?

Artist: Even in broad daylight different people see the same things differently.

Director: If that's the case even with daylight, why isn't it the case with whatever light you put things in?

Artist: What do you mean?

Director: Aren't people going to see things however they want to see them, regardless of what kind of light you offer?

Artist: Some might. But most tend to trust the artist.

Director: Trust that he's putting things in the best light, the best light for the subject?

Artist: Right.

Director: And that, of course, means that they trust that he knows the subject? Otherwise, how could he know what light is best for it?

Artist: They do trust that the artist knows the subject and what light is best.

Director: Tell me honestly, now. If the artist is bent on revenge, is he focused on what light is best? Or is he focused on what light will make the subject look worst?

Artist: Well, I suppose he's focused on what will make the subject look worst.

Director: So he violates his trust with his audience?

Artist: I guess that follows from what we're saying.

Director: Is revenge worth violating this trust?

Artist: No. But what if the light that's best really is that which brings out all of the bad qualities of the person in question?

Director: Does this person have no good qualities?

Artist: No, I suppose just about everyone has good qualities.

Director: Then mustn't the artist discover those qualities, really come to know them, then find a light that brings out the good as well as the bad — and then let the audience decide?

Artist: Decide what to think about the person?

Director: Yes.

Artist: But what if the audience doesn't come to feel about the person the way I do? What if instead of despising, it feels pity?

Director: Why would it pity?

Artist: Because it sees how the bad qualities taint the good qualities that might otherwise have been pure.

Director: Hmm. I see what you mean. But look at the bright side, Artist. Who really wants to be the object of pity?

21. Peace (Friend)

Friend: The bad taints the good that might otherwise have been pure? That's what he said? But no one is completely pure. We all have bad in us that taints our good. So does that mean we all deserve to be objects of pity?

Director: Well, if all of us are worthy of pity, then are any of us worthy of pity? But what do you think makes someone worthy of pity?

Friend: Not being at peace with himself.

Director: Being a tormented soul?

Friend: Exactly.

Director: So if Artist wants to take revenge by means of pity, he'll depict the object of his revenge as tormented?

Friend: If that person is really tormented, then yes.

Director: Tell me. Would doing wrong to another make someone tormented?

Friend: Sometimes.

Director: Why only sometimes?

Friend: Haven't you heard of people who commit wrongs in cold blood?

Director: I have. But do you think acting in cold blood means a person is at peace while he commits the wrong? Or does it just mean that he wasn't heated up into a passion?

Friend: I suppose it means the person wasn't heated up into a passion. But, then again, if you're not heated up into a passion, you're at peace — right?

Director: I'm not sure. Couldn't it be that an absence of passion actually amounts to torment?

Friend: Why would you think that?

Director: Let me give you an example of what we might call cold torment. Suppose you're with a crowd that gets worked up into a passion of excitement over something, but that something leaves you cold. Would you feel tormented?

Friend: It depends.

Director: On what?

Friend: On whether you believe it's good to get excited about that something. On whether you believe there's something wrong with you if you don't.

Director: If you don't believe there's something wrong with you, you won't be tormented?

Friend: Right. And if you do believe there is, you will.

Director: So being at peace or being tormented depends on what we believe?

Friend: Yes.

Director: Then we should tell Artist that he needs to figure out a way to portray what people believe about themselves.

Friend: We should.

Director: And how will his audience react to these people and their beliefs?

Friend: They'll pity the ones who think there's something wrong with them.

Director: Even if there really is something wrong with them?

Friend: Even so.

Director: And they won't pity the ones who think there's nothing wrong with them?

Friend: Well, if there's something wrong with you, I suppose there's reason for pity regardless of what you think.

Director: So the only ones who'll get no pity are the ones who have nothing wrong with them who don't believe there's anything wrong with them?

Friend: Right. They'll get the opposite of pity. Envy. And if that envy crosses over to out-and-out jealousy, then the acts of the jealous might just cause the ones who don't believe anything is wrong with them, when nothing is in fact wrong with them, to lose their peace.

22. COMFORT (*FRIEND*)

Friend: By helping to bring others to peace with themselves, we help bring ourselves to peace.

Director: We can really help others come to peace? Let's assume that's true. But I have a question. If we come to peace, are we comforted? Or do you think it's possible to be at peace but not in comfort?

Friend: I think it's possible.

Director: Can you give me an example?

Friend: Sure. What if you're around someone you don't like that you helped come to peace? You're at peace for having helped, but you're uncomfortable because you don't like the person.

Director: I thought we always like those who are at peace with themselves. Aren't such people good to be around?

Friend: In general, yes. But not always.

Director: So when they're not good to be around, when we don't like them, we're uncomfortable? And we're only comfortable when we like them?

Friend: Yes.

Director: But if we like them, will it bother us if they're not at peace?

Friend: Of course it will.

Director: And if we're bothered, are we uncomfortable?

Friend: We are.

Director: But if we don't like these people, will it bother us much that they're not at peace?

Friend: Honestly? I don't think it will bother us as much. But we'd still be uncomfortable because we don't like them.

Director: So we're uncomfortable either way?

Friend: Yes.

Director: But does one situation bother us more than the other?

Friend: I'd be more bothered by someone I care about not being at peace than I would be about having to deal with someone I don't like. I deal with people I don't like every day.

Director: So you're more comfortable dealing with people you don't like?

Friend: It sounds a little strange to say, but yes.

Director: Now let me ask you something. When do you think you're more effective at a task? When you're comfortable or when you're uncomfortable?

Friend: When you're comfortable.

Director: So you'd be more effective helping those you don't like than you would be helping those you like?

Friend: I suppose.

Director: And what if you more than like someone?

Friend: What do you mean?

Director: I mean what if you love the person you'd like to help?

Friend: I guess that would only make things worse. But this can't be right.

Director: What can't?

Friend: It can't be right that the more you care about someone the less effective you'll be in helping to bring him to peace.

Director: So where did we go wrong?

Friend: I'm not sure. Where do you think we went wrong?

Director: Maybe we should have said we can be more effective when we're uncomfortable than when we're comfortable. After all, when are you more likely to pay close attention to what you're doing?

Friend: You might slip up if you're too comfortable. Is that what you mean?

Director: Yes. You might doze off at the wheel, as they say. So do we have our answer?

Friend: Yes. The more you care about someone the less comfortable you'll be in working to help bring him to peace, but the more effective you'll be.

Director: And if and when that person comes to peace?

Friend: Then you'll take very great comfort in the fact — and not a little pride.

23. PLEASURE 1 (SCIENTIST)

Scientist: No, I would say that comfort and pleasure are two different things.

Director: Why?

Scientist: Because we can feel pleasure when we're uncomfortable and we can be comfortable and feel displeasure.

Director: Can you give me an example of each?

Scientist: Certainly. Suppose I'm sitting in a chair and my back hurts. I'm very uncomfortable. But then suppose the fragrance of lovely flowers wafts through the air from a nearby open window. I feel pleasure at smelling the flowers. And yet I'm uncomfortable.

Director: And the other example?

Scientist: Suppose my back now feels fine and I'm very comfortable in my chair. Then suppose I'm watching my favorite team play on television and they lose. I feel displeasure. And yet I'm comfortable.

Director: Well, you seem to have shown that comfort and pleasure differ. But now I wonder if we should prefer one to the other.

Scientist: We should always prefer pleasure to comfort.

Director: Why?

Scientist: Have you ever heard the phrase "creature comforts"?

Director: I have.

Scientist: What do you think it means?

Director: I think it refers to comforts that even animals can enjoy.

Scientist: Have you ever heard someone speak of creature pleasures?

Director: No.

Scientist: Why do you think that is?

Director: Because we don't feel the same pleasures as animals?

Scientist: Well, there are a number of pleasures that both we and animals can enjoy. But there are some pleasures that only humans can experience. These are the higher pleasures.

Director: Can you give me an example of a higher pleasure?

Scientist: Sure. We can derive pleasure from viewing a work of art. Animals can't.

Director: I see. But now I'm wondering again. If there were comforts that we can enjoy that animals can't, higher comforts — would that put comfort on a level with pleasure?

Scientist: I suppose it would, speaking hypothetically. But all comforts are creature comforts. Try and name one that isn't.

Director: What about the comfort that comes from getting a clean bill of health from your doctor after an exam?

Scientist: Animals don't have doctors, of course. But they have a way of knowing when they're healthy or sick. And I think it's fair to say they take comfort when they're well.

Director: Then what about the comfort that comes from knowing the government of the nation is in good hands?

Scientist: Many animals have leaders. And I think we can say they take comfort in knowing they're well led.

Director: What about the comfort that comes from knowing you have money in the bank?

Scientist: We can compare that to the squirrel who has a great store of nuts. Knowing he has the nuts, he is comforted.

Director: Well, Scientist, I seem to be having a hard time thinking of comforts that don't reduce to creature comforts. So it seems you're going to persuade me to prefer pleasure to comfort. But I'm not ready to give up on the notion that there may be a comfort that's specifically human, a higher comfort. If I can find it, I'll be sure to let you know.

24. PLEASURE 2 (*ARTIST*)

Artist: I can't believe you didn't think of religion as a higher, specifically human comfort.

Director: Ah, I knew I was missing something. But there are two things I'm not sure of as concerns religion.

Artist: What?

Director: One, isn't it possible that animals have religion?

Artist: Now you're being ridiculous.

Director: Am I? Two, couldn't religion be more of a pleasure than a comfort?

Artist: How do you figure that religion can be a pleasure?

Director: What is religion, true religion?

Artist: I don't know. What is it?

Director: Knowledge of the divine, right?

Artist: Yes, I suppose that's true.

Director: What do you experience when you have knowledge, when you know?

Artist: You're going to tell me you experience pleasure.

Director: Yes. That's how I figure that religion can be a pleasure.

Artist: Well, this all hinges on the question as to whether it's a pleasure to know.

Director: You don't think it is?

Artist: I don't know. I mean, what if you know something bad?

Director: What's bad to know?

Artist: What it feels like to be a criminal, let's say.

Director: I'd say it's a pleasure to know what it feels like to be a criminal — as long as you're not in fact a criminal.

Artist: How do you figure?

Director: Look at all the movies and shows on television dealing with criminals.

Artist: But they can't really let you know what it feels like.

Director: Yes, but can't they give you an idea?

Artist: Knowledge and an idea are two very different things.

Director: So when people watch these movies and shows, the pleasure derives from an idea and not knowledge?

Artist: Right, and the idea fires their imagination.

Director: So these people only imagine they know?

Artist: Well, some people know it's just their imagination. But there are definitely those who think they know.

Director: And the ones who think they know, they feel pleasure?

Artist: Yes, I think they do.

Director: But the ones who actually know, know what it feels like to be a criminal — they feel no pleasure in the knowledge?

Artist: No, I don't think they do at all.

Director: Then we seem to have established that it's not always a pleasure to know. But that doesn't mean knowing something good can't be pleasant, does it?

Artist: If it's truly good? No, it doesn't.

Director: Then what objection is there to saying there's pleasure in a religion that's true?

25. LOYALTY (FRIEND)

Director: Is loyalty always to another human being?

Friend: No, you can be loyal to an animal, just as the animal can be loyal to you.

Director: Yes, but what about loyalty to an idea? Is that possible?

Friend: Certainly it's possible.

Director: But the idea can't be loyal to you?

Friend: No, not in any meaningful sense.

Director: When we're loyal to people, don't we tend to be loyal only when the loyalty is returned?

Friend: Well, that's when loyalty is healthy. But there are plenty of times when someone is loyal but the loyalty isn't returned. And that's decidedly unhealthy.

Director: But the one-way loyalty to an idea can be healthy?

Friend: Yes.

Director: Why?

Friend: Because you get something out of your loyalty to the idea.

Director: What?

Friend: It could be many things.

Director: Can you name one?

Friend: Sure. You might get a feeling of accomplishment.

Director: Accomplishment? I don't understand.

Friend: When it's hard to stay true to an idea, you feel good about the fact that you do.

Director: So the harder the idea is to live up to, the greater the sense of accomplishment?

Friend: Exactly.

Director: Does it matter if the idea is true or false?

Friend: You mean as far as the sense of accomplishment goes?

Director: Yes.

Friend: I hate to say it, but I don't think it matters.

Director: You mean if you stay true to an idea that's true, your sense of accomplishment will be no greater than mine if I stay true to an idea that's false, assuming it's equally hard to stay to true to either?

Friend: That's why I said I hate to say it.

Director: This clearly suggests that a sense of accomplishment is not enough to steer by.

Friend: What more do you think you need?

Director: You said you get something from your loyalty to the idea. What do you get when you are loyal to a false idea, aside from a sense of accomplishment?

Friend: Not much else.

Director: But what if you have friends who are loyal to the same false idea?

Friend: And the friendship is based on that loyalty? Then you get friendship in addition to a sense of accomplishment.

Director: Those are two powerful things, aren't they?

Friend: They certainly are.

Director: Now, if you're loyal to a true idea, can you get friendship in addition to a sense of accomplishment out of it?

Friend: Of course.

Director: Do you get something more?

Friend: Yes, you get better friendships. After all, how good can the friendships be that are based on a false idea?

Director: Do you think the quality of the friendships speaks to the quality of the idea?

Friend: You're asking if we can judge ideas by the friendships they produce? I think we can. And I think the notion of so judging is in itself a beautiful idea.

26. Trust 1 (*Friend*)

Friend: But I trust my friends.

Director: Because they're loyal to the same idea as you?

Friend: Yes.

Director: Could you trust someone who isn't loyal to the same idea?

Friend: You mean this someone is loyal to an idea, but just a different idea?

Director: Yes.

Friend: A true idea or a false idea?

Director: Does it matter?

Friend: Of course it does. Why wouldn't it?

Director: Because if someone is truly loyal to an idea, any idea, his behavior is easy to predict.

Friend: And that's what you think trust is? The ability to predict someone's behavior?

Director: Isn't it? Let's put it in simple terms. If someone is erratic, can you trust him?

Friend: Of course not.

Director: What if someone is predictably loyal to an idea, albeit a false idea? Would we say he's erratic?

Friend: If he's really loyal? Then no, he's the opposite of erratic.

Director: And if the opposite of erratic, then trustworthy?

Friend: But what if he's loyal to the idea that it's good to be erratic?

Director: You mean what if he's predictably erratic? Well, that would suggest that predictability alone doesn't make for trust.

Friend: Yes. And don't we know that's true? I mean, what if someone is predictably a liar, for instance? Do we trust him?

Director: That's a good point. Then what makes for trust?

Friend: I want to say you can only trust your friends, and only when the friendship is based on mutual loyalty to a true idea.

Director: Remind me why it must be to a true idea.

Friend: Because if it's a false idea the quality of the friendship will be low, and low quality friendship never involves much trust.

Director: I see. Then tell me. What's an example of a true idea?

Friend: Honesty is the best policy.

Director: And we can trust those who are loyal to this idea, those who are honest?

Friend: Of course.

Director: But what if they're honest but ignorant? I mean, suppose you have an honest doctor who's ignorant of the finer points of medicine. Do you trust him to treat you?

Friend: No.

Director: You don't trust him because you know he's ignorant?

Friend: Exactly.

Director: But how do you know he's ignorant? Wouldn't that require some knowledge on your part?

Friend: I suppose it would.

Director: So you need knowledge in order to know whether to trust?

Friend: Yes. But there's nothing profound in that.

Director: No, there isn't. But that doesn't make it any less true.

27. VIRTUE 1 (*SCIENTIST*)

Scientist: What's the virtue of friendship? Well, what's a virtue?

Director: Can we start by saying it's a good thing?

Scientist: Of course. But that means we need to know the difference between good and bad.

Director: What is that difference?

Scientist: Let's just say that good things are helpful and bad things are harmful.

Director: Can friendship ever be harmful?

Scientist: Oh, I think it can.

Director: What makes it harmful?

Scientist: I think it gets back to what you and Friend were talking about — ideas. If your friend is loyal to a false idea, the friendship will be bad.

Director: I'm inclined to agree with you, Scientist. But something makes me wonder.

Scientist: Oh? What?

Director: If a friend is loyal to a false idea, and you know that he's loyal to it, and know that it's false — can't you try to help free him up from this false idea?

Scientist: You can. But how does this help you?

Director: Don't you think you'd make your friend a better friend? And isn't it a benefit to have a better friend?

Scientist: It is.

Director: So the question then is how to help free your friend up.

Scientist: Yes, and maybe the answer to this question tells us what the virtue of friendship is.

Director: Yes, that's a good point. Well, Scientist, what's a way to liberate someone from a false idea? What would a scientist do?

Scientist: A scientist would demonstrate that the idea is false.

Director: And how exactly would he do that?

Scientist: He'd prove that it's impossible for the idea to be true.

Director: But friendships don't take place in a lab.

Scientist: True, but we can bring the lab to the friendship.

Director: How?

Scientist: We question what our friend says and point out contradictions when he answers.

Director: But if we don't see any contradictions?

Scientist: Then we point out things he might be leaving out.

Director: Things that would make for contradictions if admitted?

Scientist: Yes.

Director: And if he sees he's contradicting himself when it comes to his idea, he'll be inclined to let go of that idea?

Scientist: In the best case, yes.

Director: But in a less than best case?

Scientist: He might hold on all the tighter.

Director: In order to prevent that, wouldn't it help to be gentle in our reasoning? I mean, do we just come right out and hit him over the head with the fact that he's contradicting himself?

Scientist: Well, we don't hit him over the head. But we do have to tell him in just so many words at some point.

Director: Then maybe we've found the virtue of friendship, or at least one of the virtues of friendship — restraint. We restrain ourselves and carefully prepare the way to telling our friend that his idea is false. But maybe we need even more restraint than that.

Scientist: How so?

Director: I'm not sure it's always best to tell our friend in so many words that his idea is false. It seems to me that it's sometimes best to let the friend come up with those words himself. After all, isn't it more convincing that way?

28. Honor 1 (Artist)

Artist: There's no honor in being told what to think.

Director: The honor lies in coming up with that yourself?

Artist: Of course.

Director: Is that because it isn't honorable to receive help?

Artist: Well, everyone needs help from time to time.

Director: Then why not help with knowing what to think?

Artist: Because you can't know what to think just because someone tells you what to think. You would just be believing what the other tells you. You wouldn't really know.

Director: But what if someone reasons it through with you so that you know all the arguments pro and con and can see why what he's telling you is true? Don't you know then?

Artist: I suppose. But what honor is there in that?

Director: There's no honor in knowing?

Artist: You don't think it matters how you come to know?

Director: I'm not sure. Tell me why you think it matters.

Artist: It matters because it means you're not original if you come to know from someone else.

Director: And originality is very important to artists?

Artist: Of course.

Director: Well, let's see. Would you like to be a great artist or an inconsequential artist?

Artist: I'd like to be a great artist, naturally.

Director: And do great artists learn everything they know from others or all on their own?

Artist: Well, they study past masters.

Director: So they come to know from them?

Artist: I suppose.

Director: And do they then simply reproduce what they've learned from these masters?

Artist: No, of course not.

Director: But you're sure they've learned something from these masters? In other words, they know something from them?

Artist: Yes, I think that's true.

Director: What do they know?

Artist: Mostly? They know technique.

Director: And do they only use the techniques they learned from the masters, or do they come up with techniques of their own?

Artist: They come up with their own.

Director: How do they do that?

Artist: By applying what they've learned, however they've learned it, to life as life presents itself to them.

Director: That's really all it takes to come up with your own technique?

Artist: It's not as easy as it seems, Director.

Director: I believe you. But does having your own technique make you original?

Artist: Of course it does.

Director: And what about having your own truth? Would that make you original?

Artist: If it's really your own? It would.

Director: How would you go about coming up with your own truth? Could it be anything like it is with technique?

Artist: You mean you might take the truth you've learned, however you've learned it, and then apply it to life as life presents itself to you?

Director: Yes. What do you think?

Artist: I guess it's possible.

Director: Now tell me, Artist. Is there honor in being original?

Artist: There is.

Director: And we agree that you can be original when it comes to both technique and truth, even though you've learned from others?

Artist: We do.

Director: Then don't worry so much about where you find your truths, my friend. Just be sure they really are the truth, and concern yourself with making them your own.

29. FAME 1 (*ARTIST*)

Director: Do you want to be famous?

Artist: Yes, but that's not all I want.

Director: What else do you want?

Artist: I want to be famous for a good reason.

Director: What's a good reason?

Artist: The quality of what I create.

Director: The good quality of what you create?

Artist: Of course.

Director: Is there an objective standard of good you hold yourself to, or do you let popularity determine whether what you create is good or not?

Artist: You know I'm not chasing popularity.

Director: But perhaps you're chasing a certain select audience, and if you win it over, that's how you'll know your creations are good?

Artist: I'm not chasing anyone.

Director: So you hold yourself to an objective standard of good?

Artist: Yes.

Director: And if you succeed in living up to this standard, you'll become famous?

Artist: Well, not exactly.

Director: What do you mean?

Artist: If no one else recognizes this standard, I'll never be famous.

Director: So in order to be famous lots of people have to recognize this standard?

Artist: Not necessarily.

Director: I don't understand.

Artist: Suppose only a handful of people recognize the standard, and suppose they think that I live up to it in my work. What do you think happens then?

Director: You're famous among that handful of people?

Artist: Yes, but famous isn't quite the right word. I'd say I'd be known by that handful of people.

Director: And if they know you, what then?

Artist: They tell others about me and my work.

Director: And those others tell others, and so on — all the way until you reach fame?

Artist: Yes.

Director: But how do you know that that handful of people who know will tell anyone?

Artist: What do you mean? It's only natural to tell others.

Director: Yes, but which others? Those who seem inclined to appreciate your work or just anyone?

Artist: Well, not just anyone.

Director: And are those who are inclined to appreciate your work many or few?

Artist: I'd have to say they're probably few.

Director: Then why do you have any hope of becoming famous? Could it be because you believe that great work must somehow necessarily win a great following?

Artist: I suppose.

Director: But don't you know it's possible that truly great work will only bring a small following — and not even, strictly speaking, a following at that?

Artist: I do, Director. And that's good enough for me.

Director: Is it? That's good. But who knows? Maybe you're wrong about those who are inclined to appreciate your work. Maybe they are many, a great many. But then I wonder whether you'd rather be wrong and famous or right and obscure.

30. Fame 2 (*Scientist*)

Scientist: But you never discussed the objective standard of good? That was the most interesting part of your conversation.

Director: Leave it to a scientist to be more concerned with questions of objectivity than fame.

Scientist: What, do you think scientists aren't concerned with fame?

Director: I'm sure some of them are. But what about you, Scientist? Do you want to be famous?

Scientist: Sure, but only if I'm famous for a good reason.

Director: And what would be a good reason to be famous for?

Scientist: To have contributed significantly to mankind's store of knowledge.

Director: And that's something that can be judged by an objective standard?

Scientist: Of course. Scientific knowledge is objective.

Director: Do you think there's such a thing as subjective knowledge?

Scientist: Yes, but I'm inclined to think it only exists in places where science has yet to discover the objective knowledge of the matter.

Director: So if I say that I know that a certain woman is beautiful, that would be subjective knowledge?

Scientist: Well, you'd say that the woman seems beautiful to you, and that would be subjective.

Director: But what if I really insist that the woman is simply beautiful, objectively beautiful?

Scientist: To be objectively beautiful, she'd have to be beautiful to all.

Director: Would she? Couldn't she be objectively beautiful to me, just as someone else might be objectively beautiful to you?

Scientist: We can say that. But then what difference is there between the objective and the subjective?

Director: Maybe science needs to discover the difference.

Scientist: And how would it do that? By means of some sort of principle of beauty that shows when someone is beautiful, objectively beautiful, to someone else?

Director: Yes.

Scientist: But wouldn't this principle entail the possibility that a man might think, subjectively, that a woman is beautiful to him when, in fact, objectively, she's not?

Director: It would. So what do you think? Would you like to be the man who discovers what makes beautiful women truly beautiful?

Scientist: I don't think you're being serious.

Director: Suppose I am.

Scientist: Well, who wouldn't like to discover the principle of beauty?

Director: And wouldn't that be a tremendous thing to be famous for?

Scientist: Yes, it would. But it seems to me that we're a long way off from being in a position to find this principle.

Director: You don't want to give yourself to a problem that you'd be unlikely to find the answer to? But couldn't you lay the foundation for others to build upon?

Scientist: Yes, but it's really not my thing.

Director: But what knowledge is more important than knowledge of beauty?

Scientist: Well, maybe no knowledge is more important. But there's plenty of knowledge that's equally important.

Director: I don't believe it. But even if you're right, would gaining this other knowledge make you as famous as you would be for discovering the principle of beauty?

Scientist: Among certain scientific circles, yes.

Director: And you'd be satisfied with that?

Scientist: Satisfied to be famous among my peers, among those who can truly understand and appreciate my work? Of course I would be, Director. Wouldn't you?

31. Success 1 (Friend)

Friend: So is he considering studying beauty?

Director: No, I don't think so.

Friend: It's just as well. I think we're a long way from finding the answer.

Director: What is this with people thinking that being a long way from the answer matters?

Friend: Who's the greater success, Director? The one who starts the work or the one who finishes it? I'll tell you. It's the one who finishes it. Maybe Scientist is close to finishing something and doesn't want to give up any time that he can spend on that in order to start something else.

Director: You might be right about Scientist. But I think you're wrong about starting and finishing. Haven't you heard the saying that the beginning is half of the whole?

Friend: I've heard it.

Director: Why do you think people say that?

Friend: Because it's hard to begin.

Director: So don't you think a strong beginning can be the greatest factor in success? In other words, can't a strong beginning count more than a strong finish?

Friend: But the finish is the other half of the whole.

Director: I suppose that would be true — if there were no middle to consider. Or don't you think there must be a beginning, middle, and end?

Friend: No, I think there must.

Director: So, if the saying is true, the middle and the end combined would amount to the beginning?

Friend: I guess.

Director: So someone successful in beginning is always a greater success than someone who merely does the middle work or finishes the effort? Or doesn't that seem right?

Friend: It doesn't seem right.

Director: Why not?

Friend: Because I have no doubt that the one who finishes is always the most successful.

Director: But why?

Friend: Because everyone remembers the one who finishes.

Director: And that's what success amounts to, being remembered?

Friend: I think a lot of people would say that's true.

Director: But wouldn't a lot of people — the ones in the middle, for instance — say that success consists in moving step by step, closer and closer to the answer to the problem?

Friend: So success is progress?

Director: Don't you think it is?

Friend: But isn't finding the answer, finishing the work, the ultimate in progress?

Director: Not necessarily. Suppose it takes a certain number of steps to solve a problem. What if the person coming right before the solution takes three steps, and the one who solves the problem only takes one? Who's made the greater progress?

Friend: The one coming right before the solution.

Director: And if progress makes you a success, who is more successful? The one who took three steps or the one who took one?

Friend: Yes, I know what you're getting at. But who gets more credit? The one who took three steps or the one who solved the problem?

Director: What do you mean by credit?

Friend: You know — general acclaim, and so on.

Director: But what about acclaim from those who know the problem and its history? Might they not credit the one who took three steps more than the one who took the final step?

Friend: I suppose.

Director: And what do the ones working on the problem care about most? General acclaim or acclaim from those who know?

Friend: Well, I know what most of them would say is most important. But I have my doubts about what many of them really crave.

32. SUCCESS 2 (*SCIENTIST*)

Scientist: Why am I satisfied with acclaim from those who know? Because any other sort of acclaim is worthless.

Director: Knowledge is the only thing that makes acclaim have worth?

Scientist: Yes.

Director: But what if acclaim from those who don't know can get you funding for research, and so on?

Scientist: If they don't know, why would they decide to give me money?

Director: Because of your reputation in the scientific community.

Scientist: My reputation among those who know.

Director: Right. The ones with the money know that in order to have a strong reputation among those who know you must be one who knows, and knows a great deal.

Scientist: And they want to reward knowledge?

Director: They want to encourage the discovery of more knowledge, and they think you'll make for a good investment.

Scientist: Why do you think they want me to have more knowledge if it's knowledge that they themselves lack? Or do you think they want to learn everything I learn?

Director: No, I'm pretty sure they don't. They want you to have more knowledge, you and your colleagues, so that they can benefit from this knowledge.

Scientist: In other words, they don't want the knowledge — they want what comes of the knowledge.

Director: Yes, that sounds about right.

Scientist: That's their measure of success — practical application?

Director: Right. And they want you to explain what those practical applications are.

Scientist: But isn't it possible for me to be greatly successful in obtaining new knowledge but wholly unsuccessful in discovering practical applications for what I learn?

Director: Yes, but isn't that when the money starts to dry up? Maybe you need a middle man, Scientist — someone who can translate pure knowledge into practical application. Wouldn't it be easier to teach this middle man what you know than it would be to teach the money men?

Scientist: Assuming he has something of a head for science? Much easier.

Director: And wouldn't he be more effective in teaching the money men the use of your knowledge than you would be?

Scientist: Yes, I suppose he would.

Director: Then here's how things stand. Success for you is knowledge. Success for the middle man is explaining how this knowledge can be used. And success for the money men is making use of this knowledge. But if you're to keep on receiving money for research, then the money men must, in some manner or other, turn a profit on the business. Right?

Scientist: Right.

Director: How do people generally turn a profit?

Scientist: By selling something that people want to buy.

Director: So we have to take the customer into account in our scheme of things?

Scientist: Yes, assuming this is the only way for me to get funding. But tell me. We've said what success is for each of the parties except for the customer. What's success for him?

Director: What else but being able to buy what he wants to buy?

Scientist: And he can't do that unless my research leads to something he wants?

Director: Isn't that how it works?

Scientist: But what if he wants it but can't afford it?

Director: Then the basic scientific lifecycle as we know it breaks.

33. SUCCESS 3 (ARTIST)

Artist: You think I'd be a success as what? A middle man? Why would I want to be that?

Director: Because you're creative.

Artist: I don't understand.

Director: The more creative the middle man, the more pure knowledge gets translated into practical application. Don't you think pure knowledge should lead to practical application?

Artist: Of course I do. But I don't like to think of myself as a middle man.

Director: But wouldn't you like to learn from those with pure knowledge?

Artist: Well, yes. Who wouldn't? But then what would I do once I learned? Teach others what I know?

Director: Yes. You'd be creative in showing them what can be done with that knowledge.

Artist: But I'm only creative when it comes to art.

Director: What's this? Don't you believe that creativity translates across fields?

Artist: If someone is a creative painter, does that mean he'd be a creative musician?

Director: Why not, if he really sets to learn music?

Artist: And if someone is a creative musician, does that mean he'd be a creative businessman?

Director: If he really means business? Sure, why not?

Artist: Are you really saying you believe that if someone is creative in one thing he can be creative in all things?

Director: I'm of that opinion, yes.

Artist: Well then, I'd like to know just what you think creativity is that it can make someone successful at anything.

Director: Well, now you've caught me.

Artist: What do you mean?

Director: I'm not completely sure what creativity is. I'm not even completely sure how to explain what I'm not completely sure about. But maybe you can help me. What do you think creativity is?

Artist: I don't have a very good definition. But I like to say that creativity involves self-expression, and self-expression makes for originality since all of us are unique.

Director: And if you do something original, does that make you a success?

Artist: Truly original? Yes.

Director: But what if someone says the true measure of success is applause, or money, or so on?

Artist: I'd say he has a bad measure of success.

Director: Then it really is enough for you to know you're doing something original? You don't need anything else to know you're a success?

Artist: No, if I could really know I'm doing something original, I'd know I'm a success.

Director: Well, you know what I'm wondering then, don't you?

Artist: Of course. You're wondering if translating pure knowledge into practical application is original work.

Director: What do you think?

Artist: I'm hard pressed to say where my self-expression would be in doing that.

Director: What's so hard? You come to know the pure knowledge, you translate it into something practical, and then you express to others what you've done. Or don't you think self-expression involves expressing what you've done?

Artist: Some would say self-expression involves expressing not what you've done but what you are.

Director: Yes, but if you aren't what you've done — what are you?

34. Despair 1 (Artist)

Director: Artist, if you translated a book from one language into another, would you be disappointed if no one read your translation?

Artist: No one? Of course.

Director: Even if you knew your work was truly original?

Artist: I'd be lying if I said I wouldn't be disappointed if no one read it.

Director: And if you translated book after book and no one read them?

Artist: I'd be more than disappointed. I'd be on the verge of despair.

Director: So would it be best, in those circumstances, not to translate any more?

Artist: Why would you think that?

Director: Because you just said you'd be on the verge of despair.

Artist: The verge of despair and actual despair are two very different things, Director.

Director: What would keep you from actual despair?

Artist: Belief in what I'm doing.

Director: Belief that the translations need to be done?

Artist: Yes.

Director: Belief that in doing these translations you'd be doing original work?

Artist: Of course.

Director: Belief that you'll one day be recognized for what you've done?

Artist: That, too.

Director: I see. But let me ask you the hard question. What if there are no grounds to believe that your translations will ever be read and appreciated? What if every indication shows that no one will ever pay any attention to them at all?

Artist: I would still believe.

Director: Why?

Artist: To keep me from despair.

Director: But what if you could translate something else instead, something that you knew would give you an audience?

Artist: But what if translating the other books is my calling?

Director: What would make it your calling?

Artist: The fact that there is no ready made audience, and therefore there is no one else willing to translate these books.

Director: The other translators aren't willing to live on the edge of despair?

Artist: Right.

Director: Do you think it's somehow good to live on that edge?

Artist: Don't you?

Director: I don't know. Most people seem to think it's good to keep away from the edge.

Artist: Yes, of course. But don't you think there's something to be said for standing on the edge and not falling in?

Director: What good do you think comes of it?

Artist: When you're on the edge, you can do things that no one else can do.

Director: If that's true, then does that mean you'd rather do things that no one else can do than live a life filled with the opposite of despair, a life filled with hope?

Artist: No, you're missing the point. The whole idea is to keep hopeful even on the edge. That's the hardest thing you can do.

Director: But why do the hardest thing, Artist?

Artist: Because the hardest is the best.

Director: What if I tell you it's harder to make a translation that will be read than one that won't, and that it doesn't involve any despair?

Artist: I suppose I'd tell you that you're wrong.

Director: You'd know I'm wrong because you've made both types of translations?

Artist: Well, no.

Director: Then before you say what's best, maybe it's best to try both ways.

35. DESPAIR 2 (SCIENTIST)

Director: Scientist, I have a question that's been troubling me.

Scientist: What question?

Director: It has to do with hope and despair.

Scientist: This sounds serious.

Director: It is.

Scientist: Please share the question.

Director: Alright. Despair is bad. Would you agree?

Scientist: Of course.

Director: And hope is good?

Scientist: Undoubtedly.

Director: So we'd do well to do everything we can to avoid despair and to live in hope?

Scientist: Yes.

Director: How do you think people usually come to despair?

Scientist: More often than not? Through disillusionment.

Director: And is this what disillusionment means? Thinking you know something important, something good, but then learning that you were wrong about it?

Scientist: Yes.

Director: Now here's where I have trouble. When you think you know something important, something good, but don't, can you feel hopeful?

Scientist: I think you can. We call this false hope.

Director: But if you learn the truth, you lose that hope?

Scientist: Yes, you do.

Director: So does that mean that if we have false hope, we should do everything we can to avoid learning the truth, in order to avoid coming to despair?

Scientist: No, not at all.

Director: Because it's good to despair?

Scientist: Of course not. It's because the truth is good.

Director: What's good about it if it makes us despair?

Scientist: The despair is only temporary.

Director: Because when we come to know the truth, we can pick ourselves up out of despair by means of it?

Scientist: Yes, precisely. And we'll be better off with the truth than we were before.

Director: I see. But will any old truth do? Or do we need the truth that gives us hope?

Scientist: You're right to ask. We need the truth that gives us hope.

Director: And how do we find the truth that gives us hope?

Scientist: Well, that's not easy.

Director: Maybe we should find hopeful people and ask them to tell us their truth?

Scientist: I suppose we could do that.

Director: You don't sound very sure.

Scientist: Some people like to keep their hopes to themselves.

Director: Why?

Scientist: Because they mean too much to them.

Director: You mean they make more of them than they should?

Scientist: No, I mean they're aware that they'll despair without them.

Director: So they say nothing about them?

Scientist: Right. Some of the strongest hopes go unspoken.

Director: That's too bad, because the ones in despair could use a little candor to help them find their way.

36. Hope 1 (*Friend*)

Director: What's it like when you're in despair?

Friend: You have no light in your life.

Director: How can you find light when you have none?

Friend: Well, that's a hard question.

Director: Why is it hard? Don't you have light in your life?

Friend: I do.

Director: Can't you tell how you found it?

Friend: It's not easy to explain. But what about you? Don't you have light in your life?

Director: Yes, I do.

Friend: How did you find it?

Director: I don't think you'll believe me if I tell you.

Friend: Try me.

Director: I found it by coming to know.

Friend: And knowing brought you light, as in the light of knowledge?

Director: Yes, and that light gives me hope.

Friend: That's not what gives me hope.

Director: Why not?

Friend: Because it's not enough to know.

Director: What more do you need?

Friend: You have to act on what you know.

Director: And that's what gives you hope?

Friend: Yes.

Director: Why?

Friend: Because nothing changes unless you act.

Director: And hope is about change?

Friend: Of course. You hope that your situation will improve.

Director: Can your situation improve through what others do, or is it always up to you?

Friend: Others can help improve your situation.

Director: Can you place your hope in what others do?

Friend: You can.

Director: So it's possible that not everyone's hope derives from acting on what they know. Some people might simply hope that others will act in a way that benefits them. But now I wonder.

Friend: What do you wonder?

Director: Must the others who act to benefit us know what they're doing? Or can they benefit us by accident?

Friend: Well, it's certainly possible to benefit someone by accident. But it's better if they know what they're doing.

Director: Why?

Friend: Because they're more likely to benefit us when they do.

Director: So if we hope that others will benefit us, we should also hope that they know?

Friend: Of course.

Director: And if we can help them know, we should?

Friend: Without a doubt.

Director: When are we more likely to help another know? When we ourselves know or when we don't?

Friend: When we know.

Director: Then doesn't it always seem, as far as hope goes, that knowledge is the key?

37. COURAGE 1 (FRIEND)

Director: Do you think it takes courage to hope?

Friend: I do.

Director: Why?

Friend: Because of what hope must push back on.

Director: And what's that?

Friend: Despair.

Director: So it takes courage to push back on despair?

Friend: Yes.

Director: What else does it take courage push back on?

Friend: Fear.

Director: What is fear?

Friend: Worry that something bad will happen.

Director: And what is despair?

Friend: Worry that something good will never happen.

Director: Would you say that courage, to the extent it's involved in pushing back on fear and despair, means knowing how to stop the bad from happening and make the good happen? Or does courage just push back blindly in a sort of wild hope of stopping the bad and bringing the good?

Friend: I don't like to say that courage is wild or blind. So, yes, I think what you said makes sense. Courage knows. But I'm not sure this knowledge necessarily means being able to stop the bad or bring the good.

Director: Then what does this knowledge mean?

Friend: It means you know what to do in the face of anything.

Director: In the face of anything? Is there any greater knowledge than that?

Friend: No, I don't think so.

Director: And if you possess this knowledge, wouldn't we have to say you're wise?

Friend: Yes, we would.

Director: To be clear, does courage make you wise or does wisdom make you courageous?

Friend: I'm not sure.

Director: Well, let me ask. Is it always wise to be courageous?

Friend: Yes.

Director: And are you always courageous when you're wise?

Friend: Not necessarily.

Director: Why not?

Friend: Because you can know what to do and not do it.

Director: So wisdom is about knowing and courage is about doing?

Friend: Exactly.

Director: If knowing doesn't necessarily make you do, does doing necessarily make you know?

Friend: No.

Director: Why? Don't we learn from what we do?

Friend: We should. But not everyone does.

Director: What stops them?

Friend: They just believe what they're doing is right and never learn from experience.

Director: Even if they experience bad consequences from what they do?

Friend: Especially then. That's when many entrench themselves in their belief.

Director: Does it take courage to get out of that trench?

Friend: Yes. And I guess this means it's clear that courage can make you wise. Because when you finally get up out of that trench, you know.

38. COURAGE 2 (*ARTIST*)

Artist: Of course you can know something but not have the courage to act on it.

Director: You have to live up to your knowledge?

Artist: Yes.

Director: Can you give me an example?

Artist: Sure. Suppose you know that standing up to a bully is the only way to get him to stop picking on you. But you're afraid to make your stand. You have the knowledge but not the courage to live up to it.

Director: But can't we say in that case you don't really know what you say you know? Maybe what you really think is that if you just ignore the bully he'll eventually go away, or something along those lines. You might suspect that making a stand is the only way to stop the bully. But you don't really know that.

Artist: Because if you knew you'd act on your knowledge?

Director: Yes.

Artist: And do you think that's always how it is? If you know, you act?

Director: It's starting to seem that way to me.

Artist: But then if you didn't act, it means you didn't know? You could say that about anything.

Director: Wouldn't it be true about anything?

Artist: But if I'm sitting on the couch watching television, and I have a pot boiling in the kitchen, and I know that if I don't get up and turn off the stove the pot will boil over, and I don't get up — didn't I know that something bad would happen but fail to act on that knowledge?

Director: No, we can say you didn't know that something bad would happen.

Artist: What do you mean?

Director: Either you didn't care that the pot might boil over, meaning you didn't think it would be something bad, or, and more likely, you forgot about the pot — and you have to remember in order to know. Or do you think you can forget something and know it at the same time?

Artist: No, I don't think that. You have to remember.

Director: So let's get back to courage. If you want to be courageous, don't you have to remember the things that necessarily go into courage?

Artist: I'm not sure what things you have in mind.

Director: The things you fear. Or is courage standing up to fears you've forgotten?

Artist: Of course it isn't. You can only face your fears when you've got your fears firmly in mind.

Director: So you must know you're afraid?

Artist: Yes.

Director: And when you know you're afraid, what can you do?

Artist: You can either stand up to your fear or run away.

Director: When you stand up to your fear, do you stand up because you know it's best to stand up? Or do you stand up for some other reason?

Artist: You stand up because you know it's best.

Director: And if you run away, it's because you don't know standing your ground is best?

Artist: Well, that's the question, isn't it?

Director: Do you think you would ever stand up if you didn't know standing up is best?

Artist: Why would you? It's hard to stand up. People look for any excuse not to.

Director: And if someone who knows what's best makes an excuse not to do it, it shows you can know but fail to act?

Artist: That's exactly the point I've been trying to make.

Director: Then I think we can say it's excuses, and only excuses, that seem to show that knowledge isn't enough.

39. Courage 3 (Scientist)

Scientist: That all sounds good. But how do we know, really know, it's best to face our fears?

Director: Maybe we need to experience what it's like not to face a fear. Once we see the alternative, we'll know.

Scientist: I don't know, Director. It seems to me that many people don't face their fears, and they never come to know what's best.

Director: You're saying many people are ignorant?

Scientist: Yes.

Director: But isn't that precisely where science comes in?

Scientist: What do you mean?

Director: I mean, doesn't science allow people to know?

Scientist: Yes, but you have to be willing to experiment.

Director: And these people are afraid to experiment?

Scientist: Deathly afraid.

Director: So we're saying it takes courage to experiment in order to prove that it's best to be courageous?

Scientist: Yes — it takes courage to know that courage is best.

Director: But can't someone prove that courage is best and then demonstrate his proof to others? Isn't that how it works with science? I don't have to experiment to know, for instance, that hydrogen bonds with oxygen. Someone else has demonstrated that.

Scientist: You're making an interesting point. But I think courage is somehow different.

Director: We each must experiment with courage and demonstrate to ourselves its truth?

Scientist: Yes. Sure, we can look to the example of others. But we'll never really know courage until we ourselves have proved its truth and demonstrated its value.

Director: Ah, its value. Maybe that's why this is different than hydrogen and oxygen? Science can teach us the truth about something but it can't teach us its value? Or can science establish the value of a thing?

Scientist: You have a point. Science can tell us the truth about gold — its physical properties. But science has little to nothing to do with the gold markets.

Director: The value of gold is determined by how much people are willing to pay for it. Is the value of courage somehow similar?

Scientist: Well, there's no market for courage.

Director: But don't we all decide, each of us individually, what price we're willing to pay for it? Some people never buy courage at all. And some people pay the highest price. Isn't that how it works?

Scientist: Yes, I suppose that's so.

Director: So, as with gold, we can tell people all about courage, everything they want to know. But in the end it all comes down to how much value they themselves place on it.

Scientist: But maybe gold is a bad example. Consider a substance like uranium. It's valuable because science has demonstrated how it's useful.

Director: So if we can demonstrate how courage is useful, we'll help to establish its value?

Scientist: That only makes sense, right?

Director: I suppose it does. But is one demonstration enough to satisfy all? Or must we demonstrate to each in a way that he can understand?

Scientist: Why not do both? Start with a general demonstration and then perform individual demonstrations as appropriate.

Director: Yes, that might be best. But there's one problem I can't quite get around.

Scientist: What's that?

Director: Are we really bold enough to set ourselves up as experts in courage?

Scientist: You don't think we have courage?

Director: I do, Scientist. But it seems to me that courage isn't something that once discovered is always yours. You have to keep finding your courage along the way.

Scientist: I agree.

Director: So let's not say we're courageous. Let's try our best to show that we're courageous. And then let's see if others can't see things for what they are.

40. Honor 2 (Friend)

Friend: There's honor in being modest.

Director: What do you mean?

Friend: I mean if you're brave, and you brag about being brave, there's no honor in that. But if you simply acknowledge the deeds you performed that involved bravery, but don't draw the conclusion that you were brave, there's honor.

Director: Why?

Friend: Because people can conclude for themselves.

Director: Any people, or do you really just acknowledge your deeds to your friends?

Friend: You're right to ask. You just tell your friends, your good friends.

Director: When you've told them, what do you do if they draw the wrong conclusion?

Friend: There's nothing you can do.

Director: So when you're modest about yourself, all you can do is hope that your friends will draw the right conclusion — that you were brave, in our example?

Friend: That's right.

Director: But what if you're too modest?

Friend: How so?

Director: You don't give them enough information to form the correct view.

Friend: Well, then you're being foolish.

Director: And is it foolish to say too much just as it's foolish to say too little?

Friend: Yes, you have to say just the right amount.

Director: So let's suppose you have three friends — one for whom what you say never seems to be enough, one for whom the smallest amount said is plenty, and one who's somewhere in the middle? What do you do?

Friend: You aim toward the middle.

Director: Yes, if you were addressing all three at once that might be best. But then the first might not hear enough. The second might hear too much. And only the third might hear just the right amount.

Friend: Yes, I think that's true.

Director: But what if you address each one individually? To the one who requires much you could say much. To the one who requires little you could say little. And to the other one, well, you could meet him in the middle.

Friend: And so I'd have a chance of being recognized by all three?

Director: Yes.

Friend: But I'm not sure it's good to address them individually like that.

Director: Why not?

Friend: It seems sort of... sneaky.

Director: Sneaky? Sneaky to address each as is appropriate to each? Tell me, Friend. Is it a mark of knowledge or of ignorance to speak appropriately?

Friend: Knowledge.

Director: And is knowledge honorable or dishonorable?

Friend: Honorable.

Director: Then let's hear no more of sneakiness when it comes to saying just the right amount.

41. BOREDOM (FRIEND)

Friend: Even knowledge gets boring at times.

Director: When does it get boring?

Friend: When you've got nothing to apply it to.

Director: Then isn't that all the more reason to seek for something to apply it to?

Friend: Sure.

Director: And couldn't the search turn into an adventure?

Friend: How? By traveling far and wide, looking for an application for my knowledge?

Director: Yes, that's one possibility. But we haven't said what sort of knowledge it is that you'd be taking with you on your travels. That matters, doesn't it?

Friend: Of course it does. I'd be bringing knowledge of people.

Director: And do you think people are the same here as they are elsewhere?

Friend: Well, I suppose that's something I'd find out.

Director: If people are the same, you just apply the knowledge you already have, the knowledge you gained here, to the people you meet there?

Friend: Yes.

Director: And what if people aren't the same?

Friend: Then I have to start learning about people again from scratch.

Director: Are you bored when you're learning?

Friend: No.

Director: And once you've learned, you're not bored when you have an application for your knowledge?

Friend: I'm not.

Director: Now help me understand something. If you're here, in this place, and you have knowledge of the people of this place — why wouldn't you have something to apply your knowledge to? Why would you feel you have to go someplace else?

Friend: Because I might already have applied my knowledge to the people of this place.

Director: And once you apply your knowledge, that's it? You're done?

Friend: Yes.

Director: So even if you travel far and wide, and learn about the people in those places, once you apply what you learn, you're done? You have to move on once more?

Friend: That's how it goes. I'm always moving on if I'm never to be bored.

Director: Well, if you get tired of that, maybe there's a way for you to settle down someplace for good, without being bored.

Friend: How?

Director: You become a teacher of what you know.

Friend: So if I have knowledge of people, I teach people about people? I teach them about themselves?

Director: Yes. Wouldn't that be a good way of applying your knowledge? And if so, wouldn't it mean you'd never be bored?

Friend: It might. But what if I have students who never seem to learn what I'm teaching them?

Director: You mean they never come to know themselves?

Friend: Yes. Wouldn't I get bored then?

Director: You might, Friend. So it seems you need one more type of knowledge — knowledge of how to find those who both want to learn and can.

42. Books 1 (*Artist*)

Artist: Haven't you ever heard the phrase "book smart"?

Director: I have. What do you think it means?

Artist: It means you're smart when it comes to what you can learn from books, but you're dumb when it comes to what you can learn from life.

Director: You can't learn about life from books?

Artist: You have to know something about life in order to learn something about life from books.

Director: So if you know nothing about life, you shouldn't read?

Artist: Well, no one really knows nothing about life.

Director: So everyone can learn something about life from books?

Artist: I suppose.

Director: And would you say that's the case with all forms of art? Everyone can learn something about life from them?

Artist: I'm not sure. It might not be enough to know something about life. I mean, you might know something about life and yet learn absolutely nothing from a certain painting.

Director: Certain paintings only speak to certain people?

Artist: Wouldn't you agree?

Director: Yes, I think you have a point. And it's like that for books, right? Certain books will speak to certain people?

Artist: I think that's true.

Director: When a book speaks to you, does that make you book smart?

Artist: No, when a book speaks to you it speaks to you about life. You learn about life.

Director: So does being book smart mean you read books that don't speak to you?

Artist: I guess it does.

Director: And you can read a book, know the book, even have much of the book memorized — and it still might not speak to you, still might leave you only book smart?

Artist: Yes.

Director: But if it did speak to you, to what you know about life, you wouldn't be book smart, you'd just be plain old smart?

Artist: Of course.

Director: So the trick is to avoid books and other forms of art that don't speak to us. But what happens in schools? We're told to read certain books.

Artist: Yes, and the books only speak to certain students.

Director: And for the other students, what's the choice? Force themselves to read — become book smart — or fail the test?

Artist: That's the choice.

Director: What's worse? To read a book that doesn't speak to you or to fail?

Artist: There's a way to pass without reading the book.

Director: How?

Artist: You find a summary of the book and rely on that.

Director: But don't teachers know about the summaries and design tests to catch those up who rely on them?

Artist: Some teachers do, yes.

Director: Then assuming we've got such a teacher, what do we do — read or fail the test?

Artist: I personally would fail the test.

Director: And what do you think of those who force themselves to read?

Artist: I feel sorry for them.

Director: Why? Won't they pass the test?

Artist: Yes, but there are other tests in life.

43. Books 2 (*Scientist*)

Scientist: Of course you have to force yourself to read at times.

Director: What times?

Scientist: Times when what you're reading is difficult. I once read a book a dozen times before I really understood what it was about.

Director: Did you enjoy it more once you understood it?

Scientist: Of course. It gave me great satisfaction.

Director: What was it like the first time you read it?

Scientist: Nothing in the book seemed to make sense. To say I was puzzled puts it mildly.

Director: I take it that when you're puzzled you, as a scientist, set to finding the solution to the puzzle.

Scientist: Yes, but I read this book before I became a scientist. In fact, the book was what convinced me to become a scientist.

Director: Would you say that the book spoke to you?

Scientist: Absolutely.

Director: Even the first time you read it?

Scientist: Something about the book intrigued me the first time. But it really only spoke to me once I read it that twelfth time. Now it speaks to me every year. I read it every summer.

Director: Can you describe what intrigued you?

Scientist: The book seemed to promise something.

Director: What?

Scientist: Knowledge.

Director: And you wanted that knowledge?

Scientist: Very badly.

Director: But let's get back to something you said. You have to force yourself to read at times. If you were intrigued by this book on your first reading, did you really have to force yourself to read it?

Scientist: Oh, yes. There were many times when I wanted to give up. I had to force myself to go on.

Director: But you were able to force yourself because you believed you'd be able to understand the book eventually?

Scientist: Exactly.

Director: What made you believe?

Scientist: Two things — faith in myself and my abilities, and trust that the author wasn't just talking nonsense.

Director: What made you trust the author?

Scientist: Just when I thought he must be talking nonsense, something would appear to persuade me otherwise.

Director: Something that spoke to you?

Scientist: Yes.

Director: And that something was enough. But do you think it's enough for everyone?

Scientist: No, I'm sure it's not. Many people do think the author is talking nonsense.

Director: Why do you think they think that and you don't?

Scientist: Because they didn't bother to understand the book.

Director: Do you think they're capable of understanding the book?

Scientist: It's hard to say. On the one hand, I'm inclined to think that all they have to do is take a scientific approach to the book and persevere in their reading. But on the other hand, if nothing in the book speaks to them, what incentive have they got to carry on?

44. Escape (Friend)

Friend: Why do many people read? They're looking for an escape.

Director: An escape? From what?

Friend: From their lives.

Director: But shouldn't a good book speak to you about your life?

Friend: I think it should. But not everyone does.

Director: Well, tell me. What about a book makes it good for an escape?

Friend: When it takes you far away, to a strange land, filled with strange people.

Director: I'm not sure a book like that would be good for an escape.

Friend: Why not?

Director: Because while I believe that exotic places and situations can make you feel like you've left your life behind, I can't help but suspect that you have a better escape when you read about people like yourself and those you know.

Friend: Why?

Director: The more familiar the characters are, the easier it is to imagine being those characters, being in their place. And the easier that is, the easier it is to escape.

Friend: Yes, I suppose there's something to that. But I think there's something to be said for having your books filled with strange people, people not like you or those you know.

Director: Strange and not like you and those you know — in what way?

Friend: People are always talking about characters' motives. Well, what if the characters have motives completely different from what you're used to?

Director: Would you want their motives to be better or worse than the ones you're familiar with?

Friend: It doesn't matter as long as they're different.

Director: And that's your idea of a good book? The motives of the characters are just different?

Friend: Yes.

Director: But what about having different motives is good?

Friend: Different motives suggest other ways of life, ways you wouldn't have considered on your own.

Director: And you consider these ways of life for yourself?

Friend: You do.

Director: But surely you don't consider the worse ways you find, do you? Isn't the basic idea to read in hopes of finding a better way?

Friend: Yes, that's true. But sometimes you need to see the worse in order to appreciate the better.

Director: When you appreciate the better, when you find a better way, that's a sort of escape, right? I mean, wouldn't you be escaping from the way you're on now if you adopted another way?

Friend: Yes, you would.

Director: And doesn't that make you the greatest of escapists? Many just go back to their lives when they're done reading. But you want more than that. You don't want to go back to your life. You want to find a better life.

Friend: And that's better than just going back to your life.

Director: A better life is better, yes. But we seem to be saying that not everyone wants a better life. How can that be?

Friend: It isn't easy to change your life for the better.

Director: It's easier to live a worse life?

Friend: In a sense, yes. But the real problem is that people don't know a better life is possible.

Director: And if they'd only read the kind of books we're talking about, they'd know?

Friend: It's not that simple.

Director: Why not?

Friend: They have to be willing to explore other ways of life. That can be scary.

Director: So people are afraid to take their escape to the next level?

Friend: Yes.

Director: Maybe you can be their guide.

Friend: Maybe. But first I need to secure an escape of my own.

45. Virtue 2 (Friend)

Director: If you want to live a better life, what do you need?

Friend: Virtue.

Director: What kind of virtue?

Friend: All of virtue.

Director: Sure, but is there one virtue that stands out from the rest?

Friend: What, you mean like some sort of master virtue?

Director: Yes.

Friend: Do you have a virtue in mind?

Director: Some people would say fairness is the master virtue.

Friend: Fairness? How can that be the most important virtue?

Director: They say you have to be fair not only to others but also to yourself.

Friend: Well, if you're fair to yourself, too, then I can see how someone might say fairness is most important.

Director: Shall we explore fairness a bit?

Friend: Let's.

Director: When you're fair to others, what's a virtue that fairness commands?

Friend: Honesty.

Director: So if someone is honest with you, it's only fair to be honest with him?

Friend: Exactly.

Director: But if someone is dishonest with you?

Friend: Then it's only fair to be dishonest with him in turn.

Director: What's another virtue that fairness commands?

Friend: Justice.

Director: You don't think justice and fairness are the same thing?

Friend: No, I don't. You can be fair but unjust. I mean, suppose you forgive a starving man for stealing a loaf of bread. Some might consider that only fair, right? But justice demands he be punished.

Director: Well, is it the same with justice as it was with honesty?

Friend: You mean if someone is just to you it's only fair to be just to him, and if someone is unjust to you it's only fair to be unjust to him? I think that's true.

Director: Is there another virtue that fairness might command?

Friend: I think there could be several. But I already know what we're going to say in each case. If someone is a certain way to us, it's only fair to be a certain way to him.

Director: Now what about fairness to yourself? Is that somehow different? What's a virtue that fairness to yourself commands?

Friend: Pride. If you do good things, fairness to yourself would mean being proud.

Director: But if you don't do good things, if you do bad things?

Friend: Then fairness would demand that you not be proud, that you be ashamed. And I can see how this goes with any other virtue we might mention.

Director: Well, let's take stock. Fairness sometimes requires that we be virtuous and sometimes requires that we be the opposite. Right?

Friend: Right. Fairness is very powerful. Not many things in this world can command opposites.

Director: Yes. But is it clear that fairness is in fact a virtue?

Friend: What do you mean?

Director: How can something that commands that we lie, be unjust, be ashamed, and so on — how can that something be called a virtue?

Friend: I have no answer to that.

Director: So maybe we need to think of other candidates for the role of master virtue?

Friend: No, I think they're all going to have the same problem.

Director: Then shall we conclude that there's no such thing as a master virtue?

Friend: Yes — but then we need to get clear on what exactly is in charge.

46. Ugliness 1 (Scientist)

Director: What is the ugly?

Scientist: The ugly? As in ugliness itself? The way a scientist sees it?

Director: Yes.

Scientist: The absence of a guiding principle.

Director: Chaos?

Scientist: Yes, chaos.

Director: But don't some people think that chaos is beautiful?

Scientist: Yes, but that doesn't make them right.

Director: Why do you think they think chaos is beautiful?

Scientist: Because it frees them of responsibility.

Director: Can you say more about that?

Scientist: Certainly. If people think something is chaotic, they figure there's simply nothing to be done about it. They throw up their hands and surrender.

Director: But you don't do that.

Scientist: No, I don't. I search for the principle that explains the seeming chaos.

Director: Seeming chaos. In other words, there's no such thing as actual chaos?

Scientist: That's right.

Director: That's a guiding principle for you, isn't it?

Scientist: It's a guiding principle for all true scientists.

Director: And the opposite of the ugly, the beautiful, is it that which acts in accordance to a guiding principle?

Scientist: Yes.

Director: So scientists acting in accordance to a guiding principle are beautiful?

Scientist: I won't be falsely modest — they are.

Director: And scientists want to see the beauty in the whole world, the whole universe?

Scientist: They do. They want to discover the guiding principles in all things.

Director: But then are we saying that the only reason why something would be ugly in this world, in this universe, is because science has yet to discover the beauty in it?

Scientist: I suppose we are.

Director: So it's possible that the days of the existence of the ugly are numbered?

Scientist: Well, yes.

Director: You don't sound so confident about that.

Scientist: If science eliminates the ugly, if science makes all things beautiful, makes them known according to their principles, there's nothing left for science to do.

Director: Science eliminates itself in the end?

Scientist: That's the conclusion I'd like to avoid.

Director: But at the same time you want to come to this end?

Scientist: Yes, I want for all things to be explained.

Director: You want for all things to be explained, you don't want for all things to be explained. Tell me. Are we a far way off from explaining all things?

Scientist: Very far.

Director: So there's no danger of science running out of things to do any time soon?

Scientist: No, no danger.

Director: Then let's keep the larger problem in mind, and if and when the day comes that we approach the end, let's hope all the beauty we've found will sustain us.

47. UGLINESS 2 (ARTIST)

Director: What is the ugly?

Artist: That which serves no purpose.

Director: So if you write a book, and you include details that are neither here nor there, that don't connect to anything else, that serve no apparent purpose — these details are ugly?

Artist: Yes. But there's a problem.

Director: What problem?

Artist: The details may in fact have an important purpose — but you're just not in a position to appreciate that purpose.

Director: So what seems ugly to one person might seem beautiful to another?

Artist: No doubt.

Director: But let's be clear. If the ugly is that which serves no purpose, is the beautiful that which serves a purpose?

Artist: Of course.

Director: But any old purpose?

Artist: No, a beautiful purpose.

Director: Then do we have to correct our definition of the ugly? We said it's that which serves no purpose. Do we really mean the ugly is that which serves no beautiful purpose? I mean, couldn't the ugly serve a purpose, an ugly purpose?

Artist: Yes, I suppose that's true. The ugly serves no beautiful purpose.

Director: Well, you know what the next question is, don't you?

Artist: I do. What makes a purpose ugly or beautiful?

Director: What do you think?

Artist: I think a purpose is beautiful when it makes you think.

Director: Is that the purpose of your art, to make people think?

Artist: It is.

Director: Are there any other beautiful purposes aside from the purpose of making people think?

Artist: None that are as beautiful.

Director: So if the purpose of a work of art, a movie, let's say, is simply to entertain, no thinking involved — how would you describe its purpose?

Artist: I guess I'd say it's a neutral purpose.

Director: So the movie would be neither beautiful nor ugly?

Artist: Right, it would just be neutral.

Director: But if the purpose were to make people think, it would be a beautiful movie?

Artist: Yes, if it really made people think.

Director: What would make it ugly?

Artist: The opposite of making people think — stifling thought.

Director: Yes, that seems to follow from what we're saying about beauty. But I wonder if you've run into this problem.

Artist: What problem?

Director: Have you ever had someone call your work ugly?

Artist: I have.

Director: Why do you think that person did so?

Artist: Because he has the opposite definition of the ugly and the beautiful.

Director: He thinks it's beautiful to stifle thought and ugly to stimulate it?

Artist: Yes, and he's far from being alone.

48. BEAUTY (*FRIEND*)

Friend: So you and Artist essentially agreed that the beautiful is thought for thought's sake? That doesn't sound very good. Thought itself should have a purpose.

Director: What do you think that purpose might be?

Friend: Life.

Director: So it's thought for the sake of life? And life is beautiful?

Friend: Yes.

Director: But what is life?

Friend: Let's just say it's energy.

Director: Thought gives you energy? How?

Friend: By clearing away the things that sap your strength.

Director: What sort of things sap your strength?

Friend: The false.

Director: So it's thought for the sake of truth, for the sake of energy, which is life, which is beautiful?

Friend: Right.

Director: How does truth give you energy?

Friend: Strictly speaking it doesn't give you energy. It helps you maintain your energy. You see, I believe we all have a certain energy by nature. The true prevents the false from interfering with that energy.

Director: So thought aims at letting our natural energy come through? And the beautiful is when this energy in fact comes through?

Friend: Exactly.

Director: That sounds good. But what do you think of this?

Friend: What?

Director: Would you say that electricity is a type energy?

Friend: I would.

Director: And what do we sometimes call this type of energy?

Friend: I don't know. What do we call it?

Director: Don't we call it power?

Friend: We do.

Director: Well, can we take it further? Can we say all energy is a type power, or just electricity?

Friend: Let's say all energy is a sort of power, and all power is a sort of energy.

Director: Then do you see what this means?

Friend: Spell it out for me.

Director: Didn't we say, if we boil it down, that energy is beautiful? Or am I misunderstanding things?

Friend: No, I think that's what we said.

Director: And if energy is power and power is energy, then isn't power beautiful?

Friend: Of course.

Director: Then I won't hesitate to say that if energy is life, as we said, then power is life. And life is beautiful. So what do we conclude once more? Power is beautiful. Or do you think our reasoning is suspect?

Friend: No, I don't. I completely agree.

Director: Well, now I think it's time to get back to the question of purpose. Are we saying it's power for power's sake? And don't say it's power for the sake of life, because we're saying that life is power.

Friend: I don't know what to say.

Director: Can life be beautiful if it has no purpose? Can the exercise of power be beautiful if it serves no end?

Friend: No, I don't think so.

Director: Then it seems we have yet to confront this ultimate, unanswered why — the same why Artist and I failed to confront when we said the beautiful is that which makes us think.

49. HOPE 2 (FRIEND)

Director: Friend, when we hope, must we hope for something in particular, or can we just have a general sort of hope?

Friend: I think we can have a general sort of hope.

Director: Then tell me. What sort of hope do you think this is? Hope that we'll understand the meaning of life.

Friend: Well, I think that's a general sort of hope.

Director: What makes you say that?

Friend: You're not hoping for something specific.

Director: What's an example of something specific?

Friend: You hope that you get a job you applied for.

Director: And it's very clear whether what you hope for comes to be?

Friend: Of course. You get the job or you don't.

Director: But isn't that how it is with the meaning of life? You know the meaning or you don't?

Friend: I don't think it's that simple.

Director: Why not?

Friend: Because you can think you know the meaning, but maybe you don't.

Director: And that's why you said hoping to know the meaning of life isn't specific?

Friend: Yes. When you hope for something specific, there's no doubt whether your hope comes true or not.

Director: In the case of what we're calling specific hopes, do we do things to make the hoped for come to be?

Friend: Of course.

Director: And what about in the case of more general hopes?

Friend: We also do things to make the hoped for come to be.

Director: But we can't be sure the hoped for actually came to be? I mean, as we said with the meaning of life, we don't really know if we know?

Friend: Right.

Director: But then when it comes to something like the meaning of life, are we just completely ignorant? Or are there signs along the way that at least tell us we're heading in the right direction?

Friend: I suppose there are signs.

Director: Would it make more sense if, instead of hoping to learn the meaning of life simply, we merely hope to find signs that will tell us if we're heading in the right direction?

Friend: Well, that would be a more specific hope.

Director: But if we go from sign to sign, and keep meeting with success, might we start to have reason to think we're coming to know the meaning of life in general?

Friend: Yes. But how do we know what the signs are? What if we think something is a sign but it's not?

Director: Are you suggesting that we can't know what the signs are unless we know what the meaning of life is first?

Friend: I am. If you don't know what something is, how can you know its signs? It doesn't make any sense.

Director: So if we're hoping for something in particular, and we get it, we might take that as a sign that we're on the right track as far as life goes, but we might not be on the right track at all?

Friend: Yes.

Director: In other words, we might have hoped for the wrong thing?

Friend: Exactly.

Director: But then how do we know what to hope for?

Friend: I wish I knew.

50. Destiny 1 (*Artist*)

Artist: I don't so much concern myself with trying to know the meaning of life.

Director: But then what do you concern yourself with?

Artist: My destiny.

Director: What is your destiny? Fame?

Artist: No, not fame.

Director: Then what?

Artist: Doing what I'm meant to do.

Director: And what are you meant to do?

Artist: Whatever the universe means for me to do.

Director: Does the universe come to you in the night and whisper in your ear what it means for you to do?

Artist: In a sense? Yes.

Director: But what does it tell you?

Artist: That's for me, and only me, to know.

Director: So only you would know if you're living out your destiny?

Artist: Yes.

Director: But what if I tell you that I think you're not living up to your potential? Would you tell me that it doesn't matter because you're living out your destiny?

Artist: Your destiny always demands that you live up to your potential.

Director: And the universe tells you what your potential is?

Artist: Yes.

Director: So as you make your way through the world, all things conspire to tell you what your potential is and what you must do?

Artist: They do.

Director: Then all you have to do is listen?

Artist: Listen and then act.

Director: And once you've acted, the universe will tell you what the next action must be?

Artist: It will.

Director: And so it goes, from action to action, on and on throughout your life?

Artist: Yes, Director.

Director: Now I'm wondering about something.

Artist: What?

Director: Does the universe tell you what to think? Or do you think on your own?

Artist: I think on my own.

Director: But the universe tells you what to do?

Artist: As I've said.

Director: So when you think, your thoughts have nothing to do with your actions, what actions you might take? I mean, the universe tells you what actions to take. Right?

Artist: It doesn't work that way.

Director: How does it work?

Artist: I have to think about what the universe says before I act.

Director: Do we all have to think about what the universe says before we act?

Artist: Of course.

Director: And the universe wants different acts from different people? I mean, we all have our own destiny to live out, right?

Artist: Right.

Director: So, to the extent we all have different destinies, the universe says different things to different people?

Artist: I suppose that's true.

Director: Then we have to make sure only to listen to the universe when it's speaking to us? In other words, we shouldn't try to eavesdrop on others' conversations with the universe?

Artist: Of course we shouldn't.

Director: What do we call those who do?

Artist: We call them interlopers, meddlers, or fools.

51. Destiny 2 (*Scientist*)

Scientist: I don't believe in destiny.

Director: But many believe in destiny, no? Why do you think they do?

Scientist: The inevitability of destiny lifts responsibility from their shoulders.

Director: You mean it takes some of the pressure off?

Scientist: Yes. Without destiny people know everything is up to them. But with destiny people believe things will simply happen regardless of what they do.

Director: Really? And are these things that simply happen good things or bad things?

Scientist: It doesn't matter. It's all part of their destiny.

Director: But then how is destiny any different than simple luck, good or bad?

Scientist: Destiny is the reason for the luck.

Director: In other words, luck isn't random? Everything happens for a reason?

Scientist: Yes. People who believe in destiny love to say that.

Director: But don't things happen for a reason? You're a scientist. Wouldn't you know?

Scientist: I do know. And yes, I do believe things happen for a reason, if in a different sense.

Director: What sense?

Scientist: The sense of the law of cause and effect.

Director: And those who believe in destiny don't pay attention to that law?

Scientist: No, they don't pay any attention to it at all.

Director: So things happen for a reason, but belief in destiny stops us from looking for the reason, the real reason?

Scientist: Precisely.

Director: What happens if we find the reason?

Scientist: What do you mean?

Director: I mean, what if we think we have a destiny and then we discover the reason behind the destiny? Do we stop believing in our destiny? Or does the reason reinforce the destiny?

Scientist: Reinforce?

Director: Sure. Isn't destiny with a reason stronger than destiny without a reason?

Scientist: I suppose.

Director: Then shouldn't we encourage those who believe in destiny to respect the law of cause and effect and search out their reasons? After all, if they succeed they strengthen their cause. But if they fail no harm is done. But now I'm wondering something about reasons, Scientist.

Scientist: What are you wondering?

Director: We said belief in destiny can lift responsibility from our shoulders. Well, I wonder if having a reason lifts or adds responsibility. What happens when you have a reason?

Scientist: When you have a reason, you have knowledge — you know.

Director: And is there responsibility associated with knowing?

Scientist: Of course there is.

Director: So the effect of finding your reason is to put responsibility squarely back on your shoulders?

Scientist: Yes, I think you have a point.

Director: But why would you want responsibility when you might have none?

Scientist: Because you can't take credit for living out your destiny if you aren't responsible for it. Otherwise it really is just dumb luck.

Director: And there's no better way to be responsible than to have a reason?

Scientist: No, none.

Director: Then let's do all we can to find our reasons why.

52. Destiny 3 (*Friend*)

Friend: I believe we make our own destiny.

Director: In other words, you don't believe in destiny?

Friend: No, I do believe in it. I believe everyone can have a destiny.

Director: But some people have destinies while others don't?

Friend: Yes.

Director: How do you go about making a destiny?

Friend: For one, you can't just be adrift in life.

Director: You have to set a course?

Friend: Yes.

Director: When you set a course do you have a specific destination?

Friend: Yes and no.

Director: I don't understand.

Friend: Your destination might be something broad. You might just hope to reach the other side of the sea, not knowing what you'll find there.

Director: You just know that your destiny lies on the other side?

Friend: Exactly.

Director: So throughout your life you keep on doing everything you can to reach that shore?

Friend: Yes, and that's how you make your destiny.

Director: What if your ship sinks before you complete your journey?

Friend: Then it was your destiny to die trying.

Director: And it's better to die trying than not to have had any destiny at all?

Friend: No doubt.

Director: So destiny boils down to trying to accomplish something. And no matter how successful you are or not in accomplishing this thing, you will have created a destiny for yourself as one who tried?

Friend: Yes.

Director: Those who don't try, can they have a destiny?

Friend: How could they?

Director: And those who try but then give up too easily, can they have a destiny?

Friend: No, they can't.

Director: So destiny requires a goal and perseverance.

Friend: It does.

Director: But is that all it requires?

Friend: What do you mean?

Director: I mean, what if you persist in aiming at a bad goal?

Friend: What's a bad goal?

Director: What's this? Do you think all goals are of equal worth?

Friend: Well, no.

Director: Aren't good goals worth more than bad goals?

Friend: Of course.

Director: So if midway through our journey in life we realize we've been aiming at a bad goal, shouldn't we try to find a good goal?

Friend: We certainly should.

Director: And is this all that unusual? I mean, how can we know what a good goal is if we lack experience with goals?

Friend: True. But some people might be lucky. They start out with a goal that's good.

Director: Yes, Friend. But let me tell you a secret about such people. While you and I might see quite clearly that they have a good goal, they themselves often can't. Doubt overwhelms them at times. So make it a point to encourage them. And don't hold their luck against them.

53. Friendship 1 (Artist)

Artist: The opposite of a political friend? That's an enemy.

Director: Do you believe such enemies can become friends?

Artist: I do.

Director: How?

Artist: Well, there are two ways. The first way is if one party comes over to the other side. The second way is if both parties move toward each other.

Director: Is one way better than the other?

Artist: Yes, certainly.

Director: The compromise where the parties move toward each other?

Artist: Of course not.

Director: The other way is best? What do we call this way?

Artist: The victory.

Director: The victory of one side over the other? Why is this way best?

Artist: In a compromise, despite what some may think, both sides are weakened.

Director: How are they weakened?

Artist: By going against their beliefs.

Director: But if one party comes over to the other side?

Artist: Then that side is strengthened.

Director: At the expense of the party that went over to that side?

Artist: Why, no. That friend shares in the strength of the victorious side.

Director: And what becomes of the abandoned side?

Artist: It loses strength.

Director: This is interesting, Artist. But tell me. Is it always belief that constitutes one side or the other?

Artist: It is.

Director: So going over to the other side always involves disavowal of belief and the adoption of new beliefs?

Artist: Yes.

Director: But isn't this always very difficult? Isn't there shame in renouncing belief?

Artist: Not if the belief you take up is better.

Director: What makes one belief better than another?

Artist: The better belief brings you strength, and happiness, and sometimes even joy.

Director: And the friends of the victory share these things?

Artist: Yes, and what better basis for friendship can there be?

Director: But will the friend who started out on the side of victory have a greater share of these things than the friend who came over from the other side?

Artist: Not necessarily.

Director: How can that be?

Artist: Haven't you ever heard of the zeal of the convert? Well, it brings its rewards.

Director: So this victory is a victory for both friends.

Artist: Right. The friends share in the victory, the victory of the better beliefs.

Director: And together they seek further victory over the opposing side?

Artist: Of course.

Director: And this amounts to winning further converts?

Artist: Yes.

Director: So what's to be done if there's total victory, if no one remains on the other side? Do all rejoice and live happily ever after, friends in what they believe?

Artist: I don't know, Director. It's hard to imagine there would ever be total victory.

Director: Why? Won't everyone eventually come to see what beliefs are best?

Artist: Well, that's the thing. If everyone believes in one thing, there will always be someone who wants to believe in something else. And then the battle once more is joined when he sets to making friends.

54. Love 2 (*Scientist*)

Director: Is there a science to love?

Scientist: Well, as we've said before, we can approach love scientifically. But is there a science specific to love? Not that I'm aware of.

Director: But couldn't there be?

Scientist: Yes, I suppose there could.

Director: What would it look like?

Scientist: I don't know. I haven't thought about it.

Director: When you try to arrive at a new science, how do you proceed?

Scientist: You don't try to take on everything at once.

Director: You start small?

Scientist: Yes.

Director: Small but significant?

Scientist: Of course. And sometimes controversial is good, too.

Director: What's a controversial aspect of love?

Scientist: Conquest.

Director: Conquest? I suppose that's as good a place to start as any. But aren't there two types of conquest?

Scientist: What types?

Director: Physical and emotional.

Scientist: Yes, I think that's true. Which of the two shall we begin with?

Director: Let's talk about emotional conquest. What is this type of conquest?

Scientist: It's when you make someone fall in love with you.

Director: And isn't love a good thing?

Scientist: Yes, but not when it's not mutual.

Director: But what if we say that conquerors always love the ones they conquer?

Scientist: In that case I suppose the conquest would be good.

Director: Because certain people never love someone back unless they're conquered?

Scientist: Yes.

Director: And just to be clear, being conquered means surrendering yourself to love?

Scientist: Well, I'm not sure about surrender. Can't you be conquered without surrendering?

Director: You mean you resist to the very end but then simply lose the battle?

Scientist: Yes. Don't you think that's possible?

Director: I suppose I do. But let me ask you something.

Scientist: What?

Director: If the conqueror loves the one he sets out to conquer, hasn't he, in a sense, lost his own battle first?

Scientist: Yes, the conqueror was conquered first.

Director: But what of those who weren't conquered? What of those who aren't in love when they set out to make someone love them?

Scientist: You're talking about seducers.

Director: Is seduction ever good?

Scientist: No, never.

Director: Now, here we are just a few steps into our science of love and we've already made a moral judgment. And there I was thinking that science is morally neutral.

Scientist: Well, science can study seducers, can say what they are, without judging them.

Director: And so if we're scientific about it, we shouldn't say that seduction is bad?

Scientist: Right. But if we're human about it, we should.

55. LOVE 3 (*ARTIST*)

Director: Is there an art to love?

Artist: Of course there is.

Director: How does this art of love differ from a science of love?

Artist: A science of love? I suppose the science would have laws.

Director: And the art of love has no laws?

Artist: No, not laws — more like guidelines.

Director: Is one of those guidelines that if you don't love someone, you shouldn't try to make that someone love you?

Artist: Ah, you're asking about the black art of love.

Director: The black art?

Artist: Yes, the forbidden art of seduction.

Director: Are you an adept of this art?

Artist: An adept? No, but I know a few things about it.

Director: How did you come to know these things?

Artist: The same way anyone does. Surely you yourself know, Director.

Director: I can imagine some things about that art. But I want to hear from someone who really knows something about the matter.

Artist: Well, how did I come to know about the black art? I learned of it when I first noticed that someone for whom I had no feelings had feelings for me.

Director: What did you do?

Artist: I tried to be kind, to be considerate, to be a friend. But that only made things worse.

Director: This person's feelings grew?

Artist: Yes. And then I thought it would be best to distance myself. Again, things got worse.

Director: What did you do then?

Artist: I sat this person down and told her the truth, that I didn't have feelings for her.

Director: And that took care of it?

Artist: No. Things got even worse still, if you can believe it.

Director: I can. But how did this instruct you in the black art?

Artist: I came to know the signs.

Director: The signs?

Artist: The signs that there's a spark of feeling and that it can lead to certain things.

Director: Let me guess. You discovered that if you blow on the spark, you can make it glow hot.

Artist: Yes.

Director: So you became a sort of arsonist of the heart?

Artist: But only a few times. I wanted to learn about the heart, to know the heart. Can you blame me?

Director: You did it all for the noble cause of knowledge?

Artist: I did.

Director: I don't believe you.

Artist: Then why do you think I did it?

Director: Oh, I don't know. Vanity? A cure for boredom?

Artist: I suppose there was some of both involved. But I stay away from the dark side now.

Director: You only encourage love when you in fact love?

Artist: Yes. But I'll tell you.

Director: What?

Artist: Reciprocated love is no easy thing to find.

56. Philosophy 1 (*Scientist*)

Scientist: The difference between science and philosophy? I'm not sure there is one. What do you think?

Director: I think science makes use of certain methods and philosophy questions those methods.

Scientist: But when philosophy questions a method, doesn't it use a method of its own?

Director: Yes, but it's just the method peculiar to the individual philosopher.

Scientist: You mean philosophy has no general method that all philosophers follow?

Director: Right.

Scientist: Well, if philosophers can check up on the methods of the scientists, why can't the scientists check up on the methods of the individual philosophers?

Director: Why would they want to?

Scientist: Why wouldn't they want to?

Director: What's at stake?

Scientist: I'm not following.

Director: If science makes a mistake in method, thousands upon thousands of scientists all around the world make mistakes, mistakes that can lead to errors in knowledge. Right?

Scientist: That's right.

Director: But if a lone philosopher makes a mistake in method, who really cares?

Scientist: I care, because there will be people who are influenced by this method.

Director: But if the philosopher isn't very influential?

Scientist: Then I suppose I wouldn't care as much.

Director: So your care increases with the success of the philosopher?

Scientist: Yes.

Director: But that's not how it is with philosophy.

Scientist: What do you mean?

Director: The care of philosophy for science remains more or less constant, regardless of how successful science is. But maybe we should check an assumption. What is success for science?

Scientist: Being able to prove that it has discovered new truths.

Director: Well, that points to a clear difference between science and philosophy.

Scientist: What? Aren't philosophers who discover new truths necessarily successful?

Director: No, I don't think they are. In fact, I think there's a prejudice against them.

Scientist: Why?

Director: Because they don't have generally acclaimed methods to back them up.

Scientist: So if they want to prove their truth, they have to prove the method that led to that truth?

Director: Yes. The philosopher has a double burden. He must prove the value of his method and then he must prove his truth.

Scientist: But can't the truth itself prove the value of the method?

Director: Well, that assumes people simply accept the truth. But if they don't, then the philosopher must prove his truth, and in order to prove this truth he must use his method, the method he used to arrive at the truth. Right? And if he uses this method to this end, he must prove the value of his method, or why would anyone listen?

Scientist: Why do you say he has to prove the value of his method and not its truth?

Director: Because he's not a scientist. Scientists tend to believe in the truth of their methods. Philosophers tend to operate on the notion that methods are either useful or not — nothing more, and nothing less. So do they cheat and use the methods best suited to prove certain desired truths? I guess I'll just have to leave it to you scientists to say.

57. PHILOSOPHY 2 (ARTIST)

Artist: So do you think philosophy is closer to being an art than a science?

Director: I suppose it depends on the type of art, no?

Artist: Let's say it's my kind of art.

Director: And what's your kind of art?

Artist: An art that speaks to people.

Director: Science speaks to people.

Artist: True, but science speaks to certain kinds of people.

Director: I thought it was meant to speak to all people.

Artist: That's what it thinks it does. But not everyone listens.

Director: And the ones who don't listen are the ones who listen to your kind of art?

Artist: Yes.

Director: Can you give me an example of something your art says?

Artist: Sure. It says there's more to the world than can be described by science.

Director: And certain people like to hear that.

Artist: Yes, very much.

Director: But what more can there be than science can describe?

Artist: Science tries to explain everything away. My kind of art says not everything can be explained away.

Director: Yes, but can you name something that can't be explained away?

Artist: Philosophy.

Director: You mean a psychologist, practicing the science of the psyche, can't say why someone becomes a philosopher, can't say there's a philosopher complex or something along those lines?

Artist: Well, that's the fear — that science can say why.

Director: Why is it a fear?

Artist: Because philosophers are fountains of inspiration for artists.

Director: And artists wouldn't like to see their fountains explained away?

Artist: Right. They wouldn't want philosophy to become prosaic.

Director: Do you think philosophy is a sort of poetry?

Artist: No, but it inspires poetry. If philosophy becomes prosaic, there's no more inspiration.

Director: So if philosophy is neither poetry nor prose, what is it?

Artist: A mystery.

Director: A mystery? But do you really think philosophers think of themselves as mysteries?

Artist: Maybe not. But to the rest of us they are mysteries nonetheless.

Director: What if a philosopher worked with an artist to make philosophy less mysterious?

Artist: I don't think it would matter. The philosopher would still be a mystery.

Director: Why?

Artist: Because no one can understand why a philosopher does what he does.

Director: Not even the philosopher himself?

Artist: I've read many explanations that philosophers have offered concerning the question of why they do what they do. None of them have helped me understand.

Director: And yet you still turn to philosophers for inspiration.

Artist: Philosophers intrigue me. Scientists don't.

Director: So art is closer to philosophy than to science?

Artist: Yes — but I'm aware that doesn't necessarily mean that philosophy is closer to art.

58. Love 4 (Friend)

Friend: When you love, Director, is it possible that you love an idea?

Director: You mean an idea of who the person is and not the actual person?

Friend: Yes.

Director: Yes, I believe it's possible. Stranger things have happened, after all. But why do you think this happens?

Friend: Because people don't allow themselves to feel real love.

Director: Why not?

Friend: Love is a very powerful feeling.

Director: And this scares some people off?

Friend: Yes. Don't you think it does?

Director: If we say that love can be as powerful as a strong tide that threatens to sweep you out to sea, then yes — I think it scares some people off. But then why substitute an idea for love?

Friend: The idea is born when people resist being swept out to sea.

Director: Can you say more?

Friend: When people resist love, do you think they tell themselves they're resisting love? Or do they like to say they're resisting something else?

Director: Hmm. That's a good question. I think most people would say love is good. So those who resist love probably tell themselves they're resisting something else.

Friend: Well, that's how the idea is born.

Director: I don't understand.

Friend: Let's say what they resist is the feeling of losing control. Won't they form an idea that control is good?

Director: I suppose they might.

Friend: Then there's the idea they love — control.

Director: But who really loves control?

Friend: Oh, I think you might be surprised.

Director: But do they call it that, a love of control?

Friend: No, they have better sounding names.

Director: So they go about with these better sounding names in search of someone who will allow them to live the idea?

Friend: Yes.

Director: But when they find someone like that, won't they love this person for being who he or she is, for being someone who lets them live the idea of control?

Friend: But that's the thing. No one ever fully lets them live the idea.

Director: So the relationship always has an underlying element of disappointment?

Friend: Yes, and that makes the person love the idea even more, by way of compensation — which only makes things worse.

Director: Well, that's an interesting psychology you're describing. And if that's how it is, then for my part I'd say it's better to be swept out to sea. But there's just one thing.

Friend: What's that?

Director: If we're going to allow ourselves to be swept away by love, shouldn't we prepare ourselves first?

Friend: How?

Director: By forgetting the ideas we may have formed about it — and learning how to swim.

59. PHILOSOPHY 3 (FRIEND)

Friend: Philosophy originally meant the love of wisdom, right?

Director: So I'm told.

Friend: Well, you know what that means, don't you?

Director: No, what?

Friend: Thinking isn't enough. You have to love.

Director: What if you love to think?

Friend: Do you really think anyone loves to think? Thinking is hard.

Director: You don't think it's possible to love things that are difficult?

Friend: Well, I suppose. But that's not really all that philosophers love, is it?

Director: No, there's more to philosophy than thinking.

Friend: So what else do philosophers love?

Director: Sometimes they love dialogue.

Friend: What do philosophers love about dialogue? The fact that it leads to wisdom?

Director: Not quite. Philosophers can love dialogue even when it doesn't lead to wisdom.

Friend: How?

Director: Let me ask you. Would you say that wisdom is like gold?

Friend: I would.

Director: If someone came around claiming to be wise, would we simply believe that what he speaks is gold, or would we test it to see if it really isn't just fool's gold?

Friend: We'd test it.

Director: Well, dialogue can be that test.

Friend: And do philosophers subject themselves to the test?

Director: Yes, though it's usually unnecessary.

Friend: Why do you say that?

Director: Because philosophers aren't wise.

Friend: Yes, yes. I've heard that a thousand times. But if you're a touchstone for gold, doesn't that mean that sometimes you'll find it? And if you find it, won't you try to make some of it your own?

Director: I'm afraid you won't believe me, but I've never been able to make the gold of another my own.

Friend: But that's impossible.

Director: Why?

Friend: We all learn from others.

Director: Learn? Certainly. But make their wisdom our own? I'm not so sure. Maybe it's possible. But it hasn't proved to be so with me.

Friend: But what do you think wisdom is that you're not able to make it your own?

Director: Do you think if I just think of it differently, I'll be able to share in the gold?

Friend: No, but everyone knows it's possible to learn wisdom from the wise.

Director: I think many believe it's possible. But what they actually learn I'd be hard pressed to say.

Friend: Well, I know it's possible. I've learned wisdom from you!

Director: Quick! Find a philosopher so he can put this alleged wisdom to the test! I'll pass no false coin to any friend of mine — from fear of the harm it might do him, and from fear of the harm he might come to do me!

60. SCIENCE 1 (FRIEND)

Director: Is there wisdom in science?

Friend: No.

Director: If there isn't wisdom, what is there?

Friend: Knowledge.

Director: Knowledge doesn't make you wise?

Friend: Well, there are different types of knowledge.

Director: Scientific knowledge is one type?

Friend: Yes.

Director: What other type of knowledge is there?

Friend: Knowledge about life.

Director: But don't scientists deal with life?

Friend: What, you mean biology? Sure, but that's not life in the sense I mean.

Director: What about the science of psychiatry? Doesn't it deal with life in the sense you mean?

Friend: I suppose.

Director: And to the extent a psychiatrist deals with life, wouldn't it be possible for the psychiatrist to be wise?

Friend: Yes, that's true.

Director: So there can be wisdom in science?

Friend: Yes.

Director: But you don't like this notion, do you?

Friend: No, I have to admit I don't.

Director: Why not?

Friend: Because science and wisdom are both better off when they're completely separate from one another.

Director: Why do you think that?

Friend: The wise often think different things about the same subjects. But scientists, when something has been demonstrated, agree. So it's obvious the two don't belong together.

Director: But can't the wise demonstrate their wisdom? Can't they compel agreement?

Friend: How do you prove to a certainty what you know about something like happiness?

Director: You mean happiness is a fitting subject for wisdom but not for science?

Friend: If it were a fitting subject for science, we'd have no need for the wise.

Director: So you believe there will always be a need for the wise since there are subjects that will never be fitting for science?

Friend: Yes, I do.

Director: But how do we know what questions are or aren't fitting for science?

Friend: We know when science can't give a persuasive answer to a question.

Director: But what if science can't do so simply because it has yet to learn the answer?

Friend: It's not inevitable that science will come to know all things, Director.

Director: No, I agree. But don't you think it should try?

Friend: Sure, but for every one thing it learns about something like happiness, ten new questions appear.

Director: Questions that wisdom might be able to answer?

Friend: Yes.

Director: Then it seems science and wisdom can make a good team.

Friend: Maybe. But what happens when science finds a new answer and it goes counter to the answers of the wise?

Director: Then wisdom must either directly challenge science or simply accept the new answer, as any scientist would, and move on to address the ten new questions that appear. I'll let you guess which alternative I think best.

61. SCIENCE 2 (ARTIST)

Director: So where do you think an artist should focus? On things that are known or on things that are yet to be known?

Artist: I have to object to your question. How do we know that what we don't know we'll eventually know?

Director: You don't believe that science can conquer all?

Artist: Oh, I believe science is powerful and conquers much. But what if it's asking the wrong questions?

Director: What do you mean?

Artist: Suppose science is moving forward like a car with its headlights on in the night. Sure, it brings light as it goes — but what about all the darkness off to the sides? If it just keeps on moving forward these sides will always remain in the dark. And that's to say nothing about what's behind.

Director: So science should ask the questions pertaining to the sides and the rear?

Artist: Yes, of course.

Director: Well, maybe that tells us the answer concerning art.

Artist: What do you mean?

Director: Art can try to steer science toward these dark areas.

Artist: How can it do that?

Director: How else? By concerning itself with the fringe between light and dark.

Artist: So what does an artist do? Just plant himself there on the fringe and call for people to pay attention?

Director: More or less? Yes.

Artist: But what's to say that science will pay any attention to art?

Director: Before I answer that, let me ask. Do you believe science requires imagination?

Artist: Well, the theoretical aspect of science does.

Director: And who generally sets the direction of science?

Artist: The theorists.

Director: If you could capture the imagination of the theorists, what might you do?

Artist: Influence the direction of science.

Director: So how do you capture the imagination?

Artist: It depends on the individual.

Director: Suppose this individual dedicates his life to bringing light to darkness. How would you get his attention?

Artist: By showing him that the darkness to the sides and behind is as urgently in need of light as the darkness in front.

Director: And how would you do that?

Artist: I suppose I'd have to show the danger in not confronting this darkness.

Director: How?

Artist: What if I started out on the edge of the darkness, as you suggested — and then disappeared into it?

Director: What would that accomplish?

Artist: The scientist might want to rescue me.

Director: And if others follow you into the darkness?

Artist: The situation only becomes more urgent.

Director: So you'd want others to follow you?

Artist: Well, I don't really want to be the man who leads people off into the dark.

Director: Not even if it's for a good cause?

Artist: The cause of light is no good if it requires bringing others into the dark.

Director: Then you must go alone. Disappear into the darkness, Artist. But never allow yourself to lose sight of the light. And never stop making as much noise as you can, so you can be sure that science knows where to look — and that it won't forget about you while it's focused on driving straight ahead.

62. Friendship 2 (Scientist)

Scientist: Yes, I think art can be a friend of science.

Director: But what does it mean to be a friend? Don't you have to have shared interests?

Scientist: Yes, certainly.

Director: So what do art and science share?

Scientist: A love of truth.

Director: Science loves to find truth and art loves to depict it?

Scientist: Precisely.

Director: But what if it's the other way around?

Scientist: What do you mean?

Director: What if art finds truth and science depicts it?

Scientist: How does art find truth?

Director: The same way science does — except without a scientific method.

Scientist: And how does science depict this so-called truth?

Director: Through scientific method. Art finds the truth and science proves it's true.

Scientist: And you think science and art can be friends on these terms?

Director: Why, yes — unless science is jealous of art.

Scientist: This is ridiculous. Art should be jealous of science.

Director: Why? Because science is tethered by its method?

Scientist: And artists proceed with no method?

Director: Oh, they have method. But it's a method unique to the artist.

Scientist: You really think each artist has his own method?

Director: Each true one does.

Scientist: But then you must think there are few true artists.

Director: Very few.

Scientist: But you believe there are many scientists?

Director: Yes. Don't you?

Scientist: I think you're teasing me, trying to make me feel like art is a more exclusive club than science.

Director: Isn't it?

Scientist: Let's say it is. What then?

Director: Would you still be friends with artists, knowing that they're more rare?

Scientist: I suppose you'll tell me I should feel honored to have such rare men as friends.

Director: Shouldn't you?

Scientist: And what about the artists? Should they feel honored to have scientists as their friends?

Director: Yes.

Scientist: Why?

Director: Because a friend, a true friend, is always a great honor to have. No?

Scientist: Well, yes, of course.

Director: So wouldn't you agree that if science wants this honor it should make a point of befriending art?

Scientist: Yes, but shouldn't art also make a point of befriending science?

Director: Of course. But I think it's up to science to make the first move.

Scientist: Oh? Why do you think that?

Director: Because science is generally more confident than art. Or do you think I'm mistaken, and art is more confident than science?

Scientist: No, I think you're right. Science has good reason to be more confident than art.

Director: Then put that confidence to use, my friend. And see if it can't be the basis for a lasting bond.

63. ART (SCIENTIST)

Scientist: He said that good art destroys boundaries.

Director: Do you believe him?

Scientist: Well, there's more. He said that good science delineates boundaries.

Director: Is he right about that?

Scientist: In a sense, I suppose. But in another sense he couldn't be more wrong.

Director: Good science destroys boundaries?

Scientist: Truly creative science can, yes.

Director: So art and science aren't simply opposites, the one making boundaries the other wrecking them?

Scientist: No, I don't believe they are.

Director: In fact, can't art help to establish boundaries?

Scientist: How so?

Director: Why, by only presenting things within certain limits.

Scientist: Yes, that's true.

Director: And can't an artist's proud notion of destroying boundaries at times be silly?

Scientist: Silly? Why? What do you mean?

Director: Aren't these boundaries always boundaries that are ready to be done away with?

Scientist: In what sense?

Director: In the sense that we don't need them anymore.

Scientist: Can you say more?

Director: Well, look at it this way. How does an artist destroy a boundary?

Scientist: By going beyond that boundary.

Director: Does the boundary no longer exist just because some artist went beyond it? I mean, if I step across the boundary between my property and yours, have I destroyed the boundary?

Scientist: No, the boundary still exists.

Director: But if from that moment forward a great many people follow my lead and step across the boundary and keep stepping across, moving back and forth as a matter of course?

Scientist: Then the boundary doesn't mean very much.

Director: Would I have destroyed the boundary?

Scientist: In a sense? Yes.

Director: But without the others?

Scientist: Then you wouldn't have destroyed the boundary.

Director: Isn't it the same with artists? Don't they need people to follow them across the boundary in order to destroy that boundary?

Scientist: Yes, of course.

Director: And if an artist crosses a boundary that others aren't ready to cross?

Scientist: He won't have any effect on the boundary, or at least only very little.

Director: So an artist who wants to destroy must find a boundary that people are ready to cross, one they don't need any more?

Scientist: Yes, I suppose that's true.

Director: What do you think happens to those who cross boundaries that people are far from being ready to cross?

Scientist: I think they're viewed as crazy, and might well be crazy — though one day people might think of them as visionaries.

Director: But what happens to scientists who cross such boundaries?

Scientist: Nothing. They can prove why crossing the boundary isn't crazy.

Director: Well, there's something to be said for that.

64. Life 1 (Scientist)

Director: What is life?

Scientist: Do you want the scientific definition?

Director: No, I can look that up. I want your definition.

Scientist: How do you know my definition isn't the scientific definition?

Director: Because I know you, Scientist.

Scientist: Well, you're right. But I'm going to disappoint you. I have notions about life, but I don't have a strict definition.

Director: Why don't you have a strict definition? Is life too big a topic for you to take on?

Scientist: It's not that. I just don't think life admits of a strict definition.

Director: Why not?

Scientist: Because we need room to grow.

Director: We humans?

Scientist: Yes.

Director: Well, what notions do you have that allow us room to grow?

Scientist: For one, the human isn't limited by the body we're familiar with.

Director: We can modify the body?

Scientist: Yes, of course. We're already doing this.

Director: But isn't there a point at which we've modified the body such that it's no longer human?

Scientist: That's where I want to say no.

Director: You'd allow for infinite modification?

Scientist: I would.

Director: Even to the brain?

Scientist: Even to the brain.

Director: Then what makes us human?

Scientist: The chain.

Director: The chain?

Scientist: Yes, the history that keeps us linked to our human ancestors.

Director: I see. But what happens if someone doesn't keep to human history?

Scientist: How would that be possible? Any change to the human is a part of human history.

Director: Yes, but what if the change isn't to the human?

Scientist: What do you mean?

Director: What if a scientist works with other species, and works with them in a way that brings them into close convergence with the human?

Scientist: Why would he do that?

Director: To stand outside of human history.

Scientist: But that's crazy.

Director: However that may be, what if his end product strongly resembles whatever it is we're calling human? Would it be human?

Scientist: No. The human must develop from within the human, not from outside.

Director: Science must bind itself with the historical chain?

Scientist: Yes. Because if it doesn't, then anything goes.

65. LIFE 2 (ARTIST)

Artist: Life? I only hope my art enhances it.

Director: How can it do that?

Artist: If all goes well? By making people feel more alive.

Director: But what does it mean to feel alive?

Artist: You don't know?

Director: I know what it means to be happy. I know what it means to be sad. Both are part of life. So does that mean that your art makes people feel both more happy and more sad?

Artist: Yes.

Director: You surprise me, Artist. I thought you were going to say your art only makes people feel more happy.

Artist: Why would I say that? My art deals with life — all of life.

Director: But why would people want to feel more of all of life? Don't they have enough of the bad things in life all on their own?

Artist: The bad puts the good into high relief and makes it beautiful.

Director: And people accept the bad for the sake of the beautiful?

Artist: My audience does.

Director: Who is your audience?

Artist: Anyone who can appreciate my art.

Director: And appreciation leads to the enhancement of life?

Artist: Yes, it does.

Director: Tell me. How exactly does one appreciate art?

Artist: To really appreciate it? You have to feel what the artist intends.

Director: But what if the artist has no intent?

Artist: That's not possible. There's always intent behind art.

Director: Because even to intend nothing is a sort of intention?

Artist: Yes.

Director: But your intent is to make people feel more alive?

Artist: That's right.

Director: And you execute your intent by presenting the good and bad in life in contrast to one another?

Artist: I do.

Director: Now, if that's all you do, what's hard for your audience to appreciate? Can't everyone tell the difference between the good and the bad?

Artist: Not everyone has the same notion of good and bad.

Director: So someone with a different notion of things might think that the good you present is bad, and the bad good?

Artist: Yes, that's true. I can't help what people think.

Director: But can't you? For some people at least?

Artist: And how would I do that?

Director: Why, you could hang signs on things. This is beautiful. This is good. This is ugly. This is bad. Can't you do that?

Artist: Of course I can.

Director: Then why not do it?

Artist: Because art is most powerful, makes you feel most alive, not when it tells you what to think but when it makes you think. And what's more worth thinking about than the difference between the beautiful and the ugly, the bad and the good?

66. PETS 2 (*SCIENTIST*)

Director: How would you define a pet?

Scientist: As an animal that's been domesticated.

Director: Don't we sometimes refer to humans as pets?

Scientist: Yes, sometimes.

Director: What would it mean to be a human pet? To be a human that's been domesticated?

Scientist: Of course not.

Director: Because all humans are domesticated?

Scientist: Well, I'm not so sure about that.

Director: There are wild human beings?

Scientist: Yes.

Director: The wild human beings can't be pets?

Scientist: No, they can't.

Director: Then what's a human pet?

Scientist: I think it's someone who's pampered and spoiled.

Director: Now, with animals we can have pets that aren't pampered and spoiled, can't we?

Scientist: Yes, I suppose that's true.

Director: But human pets are always spoiled?

Scientist: Yes.

Director: And if we stop spoiling humans, they stop being pets?

Scientist: Well, it's not so simple. Once spoiled, you're pretty much always spoiled.

Director: You mean that if we stop spoiling someone, he won't revert to being wild?

Scientist: I don't think anyone who has ever been a spoiled pet can become wild.

Director: Why is that?

Scientist: Because someone who was a pet wouldn't survive in the wild.

Director: He wouldn't be tough enough?

Scientist: Right.

Director: What about an animal pet? How would it do in the wild?

Scientist: I think it would have a very hard time.

Director: But it might be able to survive?

Scientist: It might, depending on the animal.

Director: Well, if an animal can survive, why can't a human? Aren't humans resourceful?

Scientist: Spoiled humans aren't.

Director: Why not?

Scientist: Because they've never had reason to be resourceful.

Director: But what if they resisted being spoiled? Wouldn't they have had a need to be resourceful then?

Scientist: Don't you think it's rare for someone who is being spoiled to resist?

Director: Rare, but possible.

Scientist: What do you think such a person would have to do?

Director: He'd have to take on difficult things, things that really make him work. In fact, maybe science could be such work. Doesn't science make real demands on a person?

Scientist: It certainly does.

Director: And unlike some things, isn't science clear about when these demands aren't met?

Scientist: Very clear.

Director: Then maybe science can give a person like this a chance, a chance to prove that he's willing to work and that he's able to meet the demands.

Scientist: But what if he works but can't meet the demands?

Director: Can't? Then we have to hope that his time with science will have taught him what sort of work is more properly his own.

67. Pets 3 (Artist)

Artist: Humans and their pets need to be well matched.

Director: How can you tell if they're well matched?

Artist: Both pet and human thrive.

Director: Is it just a matter of trial and error, or is there a science to having a good match?

Artist: I think it's more of an art than a science.

Director: Why?

Artist: Because you need to know what sort of human and what sort of pet you're dealing with, and humans and pets don't fit neatly into scientific types.

Director: What sort of types do they fit into?

Artist: General types.

Director: You mean, as far as humans go, types like patient and impatient?

Artist: Sure.

Director: And if the human is patient, the match is more likely to be a success?

Artist: Yes.

Director: The more good qualities the human has in general, the more likely there will be success?

Artist: That's right.

Director: But what about the pet? Doesn't it need to have good qualities, too?

Artist: Of course.

Director: Then do we simply match good with good?

Artist: Well, it's not that simple.

Director: Why not?

Artist: How many people do you think have the good qualities we want?

Director: Well, not as many as we might like.

Artist: And don't you think it's the same with pets?

Director: I suppose it would be.

Artist: That means not all our matches will be perfect.

Director: Is that a surprise?

Artist: No, but it means we have to accustom ourselves to matches that aren't perfect — many of them.

Director: I agree.

Artist: But you do see the problem, don't you?

Director: What problem?

Artist: The people can't know their matches are less than ideal.

Director: Why not?

Artist: Because then they might not appreciate their pets as much.

Director: I'm not sure I agree with that line of thinking.

Artist: Would you tell them their matches are less than ideal?

Director: Don't you think many of them will be able to figure that out on their own? And if they do, isn't that to the good?

Artist: How do you figure?

Director: Knowing the match isn't perfect is the first step to doing something about it.

Artist: You mean the human will try to improve in order to have a better relationship with the pet?

Director: I would. Wouldn't you?

Artist: Yes.

Director: And if the human improves, might the pet not follow the lead and improve, too?

Artist: You have a point.

Director: Then isn't it clear that working together to improve is much better than believing your match is ideal when it's not?

Artist: It is to me. But it's also clear that it's easier to believe than to work.

68. Ideas 1 (Artist)

Director: Artist, do you work ideas into your art?

Artist: Yes, of course.

Director: How do you do it?

Artist: How? I just do it.

Director: If we think of your art as a house, where do ideas figure in? Are they the foundation, the frame, the roof, the floors? Or maybe they're the electrical work or the plumbing? Or the windows or the paint? What?

Artist: They're all of that.

Director: Then is there any part of the house that isn't made up of ideas?

Artist: No, and the entire house itself is one big idea.

Director: An idea made up of ideas?

Artist: Yes.

Director: But won't that get confusing?

Artist: Not if all of the ideas work together in harmony.

Director: Do your ideas always work together in harmony?

Artist: Well, here's the thing. Sometimes you want a little dissonance in your work.

Director: Why?

Artist: Perfect harmony can be boring.

Director: But didn't you just say anything less than harmony can be confusing?

Artist: I did.

Director: So you want your work to be confusing?

Artist: Yes, to some degree. That keeps it interesting for my audience.

Director: But if the goal is to communicate ideas, wouldn't you do that more effectively without the confusion?

Artist: Yes, but communicating ideas isn't the only goal.

Director: What else do you try to achieve?

Artist: You want your audience to build a house of their own.

Director: A house made up of ideas?

Artist: Yes.

Director: And just to be clear, you don't want them to move into your house?

Artist: No, I don't. My house is an ideal house. People need houses they can actually live in.

Director: And the dissonance you build into your house discourages people from moving in?

Artist: Right. They're a bit confused by my house and think twice about trying to live in it.

Director: But it's nice to look at and get some ideas from? And they can get other ideas, similarly, from somewhere else?

Artist: Yes, they can.

Director: When people take ideas from here and there, isn't there a risk that they won't go well together?

Artist: Of course there is.

Director: Have you ever considered consulting with people to help them select appropriate ideas?

Artist: I don't want that responsibility.

Director: Why not?

Artist: Because what if I'm wrong and they're not happy in their home? I couldn't bear the thought, Director. So I don't tell anyone what to do. I just suggest to them what's possible and leave them to their own devices.

69. Ideas 2 (Scientist)

Scientist: What's possible? Of course science is concerned with that.

Director: So science knows what's possible? Or does science just have an idea of what's possible?

Scientist: Sometimes science knows; sometimes science has an idea.

Director: And when we talk about the possible, we're not just talking about what's possible for rocks and metals and so on. We're talking about what's possible for human beings, right?

Scientist: Of course. Science is concerned with all things and with human beings especially.

Director: Now, when would science tell a human being what's possible in that human's own life? When science knows what's possible or when it only has an idea?

Scientist: Well, it's difficult to say what's possible for any given human being.

Director: Difficult but not impossible?

Scientist: Yes, true.

Director: So when does science speak up?

Scientist: Science speaks when it knows.

Director: And it might not be very often that it knows what's possible for another?

Scientist: That's right.

Director: When would science speak if it only has an idea of what's possible?

Scientist: I don't think science should speak then. It would be irresponsible.

Director: But what if the person in question is desperately in need of some advice? What if the person is in a crisis? Wouldn't science be compelled to speak even if it only has an idea?

Scientist: Here's the problem, Director. Not only does such speech put the person in question at risk, this speech damages the authority of science.

Director: You mean if science only speaks what it knows, its authority remains intact? But if it speaks when it doesn't know, and it becomes clear that it doesn't know, people won't listen when it speaks what it knows?

Scientist: Precisely.

Director: But, Scientist, aren't there times when a person truly stands in need of an idea?

Scientist: If that's true then that person can get his idea from somewhere else — from art, for instance.

Director: Have you ever had to depend upon an idea?

Scientist: I have.

Director: Did you get it from art?

Scientist: No, I didn't.

Director: Where did you get it from?

Scientist: My high school science teacher.

Director: What did he say?

Scientist: Something very simple but to me very powerful. He said there's something noble about science.

Director: Did you believe him?

Scientist: I did.

Director: This idea of the noble in science, has it served you well?

Scientist: It has, Director.

Director: And now do you know that science is noble, or do you still just have an idea?

Scientist: Now I know.

Director: So it seems you turned an idea into knowledge. Why not give someone else the chance to do the same?

70. Ideas 3 (Friend)

Friend: Turning ideas into knowledge? I guess you just have to live the idea.

Director: What if it's a bad idea?

Friend: What do you mean?

Director: I mean, what if you think something is noble, for instance, but the truth is that it's not?

Friend: Well, if you live that idea, thinking the thing in question is noble, don't you make it noble?

Director: I don't know, Friend. I can think I'm ten feet tall and live that idea my whole life, but that doesn't make me ten feet tall — it makes me crazy.

Friend: Yes, but what if the idea is that it's noble to think you're ten feet tall even though you're not?

Director: Don't you think ideas have to correspond to reality?

Friend: Not necessarily. In fact, I think a lot of people have ideas that don't.

Director: But shouldn't ideas correspond to reality?

Friend: Of course — but what's reality?

Director: Do you think you're ten feet tall?

Friend: No. But what if you and I decide to believe that we're ten feet tall? And what if we persuade all of our friends to believe they're ten feet tall? And they persuade all of their friends. And so on. Might it not get to the point where we actually change the way we measure things? Might it not get to the point where the tape measurers will say that we are in fact ten feet tall? Do you see what I'm driving at?

Director: Yes, I do. But in the meantime I'm pretty sure that if you go around saying you're ten feet tall, people will think you're crazy.

Friend: Maybe that's the price you have to pay in order to turn an idea into knowledge.

Director: But why would people want to believe they're ten feet tall?

Friend: Why? Because it's flattering.

Director: But if we get to the point where we change the way we measure feet, then it's not flattering anymore.

Friend: True, but that's just the way it goes. The early adopters of an idea like to think they're special. By the time everyone else catches up, they've already moved on to another new idea.

Director: How long does this catching up take?

Friend: For big ideas? It can take centuries.

Director: So early adopters won't necessarily move on to other ideas? They might spend their whole lives living the idea, making it knowledge?

Friend: Yes, and by the time the idea has become common knowledge, other new ideas will be in play.

Director: But why are you so sure that it will happen that way?

Friend: What do you mean?

Director: What if the idea becomes common knowledge and there are no new ideas, at least no new ideas that challenge the common knowledge?

Friend: There will always be ideas to challenge common knowledge.

Director: Perhaps. But what if these challenger ideas don't catch on? Or are they guaranteed to catch on?

Friend: Well, it depends on the idea.

Director: Do you think being flattering is enough for an idea to catch on and take on something as powerful as common knowledge?

Friend: Do you?

Director: No. I think something more is needed. The idea must somehow tap the strength of those who believe in it, must bring that strength out. Doesn't that make sense?

Friend: Yes. And then that's the reality to which an idea must correspond, the reality of that latent strength.

71. TRUST 2 (SCIENTIST)

Scientist: You have to be careful when it comes to trusting scientists who have big ideas.

Director: Why?

Scientist: Because they can be blinded by them.

Director: How so?

Scientist: They can focus so exclusively on their ideas that they don't see anything else.

Director: What should they focus on?

Scientist: Facts.

Director: But don't scientists with big ideas focus on the facts that support their ideas?

Scientist: That's the thing. Those might be the only facts they focus on. They might ignore other important facts.

Director: And when they do that that's when you can't trust them?

Scientist: Precisely.

Director: Then you know what to do, don't you?

Scientist: Call attention to the troublesome facts?

Director: Yes.

Scientist: But I could spend my entire career doing that.

Director: Wouldn't that be a career well spent?

Scientist: I don't know, Director. Where would that leave me?

Director: What do you mean?

Scientist: I mean what about my ideas?

Director: You have big ideas?

Scientist: No, I have reasonably sized ideas.

Director: What makes them reasonably sized?

Scientist: The fact that they don't blind me to problematic facts.

Director: What do you want to do with these ideas of yours?

Scientist: What else? Prove that they're true.

Director: So to you, ideas and hypotheses are the same thing?

Scientist: Of course.

Director: What makes you pick a certain hypothesis?

Scientist: Something about the facts I observe suggests it to me.

Director: So you trust the facts when you make your hypothesis?

Scientist: Yes.

Director: And when you work to test your hypothesis, does that trust sustain you?

Scientist: Of course it does.

Director: But scientists with big ideas, what sometimes happens with them?

Scientist: They trust the facts, but they have an unwarranted trust.

Director: What makes it unwarranted?

Scientist: They make big leaps from the facts in arriving at their hypotheses.

Director: So often they're wrong?

Scientist: Yes.

Director: But sometimes they're right?

Scientist: True.

Director: Once they know one way or other, can you trust them then?

Scientist: I'd like to say yes, but these people are gamblers, Director. Win or lose, they almost always go right back up to the table and place another large bet. They're addicts. And how much trust do you think an addict deserves?

72. TRUST 3 (*ARTIST*)

Artist: Scientist told you to be careful trusting scientists with big ideas? But what about the great theorists?

Director: I don't know, Artist. It's possible he somehow distinguishes them from the ones he was complaining about.

Artist: Or maybe he was just in a mood and didn't really mean what he said.

Director: Maybe. But what about you? Do you trust artists with big ideas?

Artist: Why limit it to artists? Why not ask whether I trust anyone with big ideas — scientists, businessmen, politicians, etcetera?

Director: Well, do you?

Artist: It depends.

Director: On what?

Artist: On two things. One, how dedicated they are to their big idea. And two, how much I stand to gain from it.

Director: That's a refreshingly honest answer. But really, Artist, mustn't there be a third thing?

Artist: And what would that be?

Director: How likely it is the idea will come true.

Artist: A good point.

Director: So you trust those with ideas that would benefit you that are likely to succeed?

Artist: Yes.

Director: Now let's forget about ideas, big or not. Would it ever make sense to say that you can trust someone who is simply unsuccessful in what he does?

Artist: Of course it would. Someone who is unsuccessful can be a man of virtue — honest, and so on.

Director: But if the unsuccessful man isn't a man of virtue?

Artist: Then I wouldn't trust him.

Director: Could someone be highly successful and not virtuous?

Artist: Yes, and I wouldn't trust him, either.

Director: You wouldn't trust in his success?

Artist: What are you driving at?

Director: Wasn't there something that made him successful?

Artist: Sure. It could have been ruthlessness, craftiness, an ability to lie persuasively.

Director: But you believe that honesty, and so on, is always the best policy, even though it doesn't always lead to success?

Artist: You're asking whether it's better to choose honest failure over dishonest success?

Director: Yes. What do you think?

Artist: I have to say it's better to choose honesty.

Director: You have to say it because you don't want to seem immoral, or you have to say it because it's true and you always say what's true?

Artist: It's true.

Director: Now, here's the hard question. Suppose you need something to succeed very badly. Would you choose the honest failure or the dishonest success to carry out the task?

Artist: I would do it myself.

Director: A good answer. You trust yourself.

Artist: Of course I do.

Director: Is it a virtue to trust yourself?

Artist: It depends on what it is in you that you trust. If you trust in something good, then that trust is good, is a virtue. But if you trust in something bad? Well, that makes you a different sort of person.

73. TRUST 4 (FRIEND)

Friend: But why would you ever trust in something bad? That doesn't make sense.

Director: Why not?

Friend: What makes it bad? If it brings good results, isn't it good?

Director: What do you think of as good results?

Friend: Happiness, things like that.

Director: So if something makes you happy, it can't be that bad?

Friend: Right — if you're truly happy.

Director: Then you would say to trust in your own happiness?

Friend: Yes.

Director: And what about the happiness of others? Do you trust in that?

Friend: What do you mean?

Director: What if they do something that makes them happy? Is that thing good?

Friend: Good for them.

Director: But not necessarily good for you?

Friend: Not necessarily. When you say you should trust in your own happiness, part of what you're really saying is that you shouldn't allow what makes others happy to affect you unduly. Otherwise you're trusting in what they trust in to make yourself happy.

Director: And that trust is misplaced?

Friend: Definitely. We have to trust in what makes us happy, not others.

Director: Why do you think people trust in what makes others happy?

Friend: Because they don't know how to make themselves happy.

Director: And how can they learn how to make themselves happy?

Friend: By being very quiet and keeping very still.

Director: So they can hear themselves think?

Friend: Yes, but first they need to hear what will make them happy. Once they've heard that then they think, think how to obtain their happiness.

Director: But what if you hear that you want what makes others happy?

Friend: No one really hears that.

Director: Then why do they get the idea?

Friend: They get it because it's hard to make yourself happy.

Director: So rather than trust what I want I trust what others want, and that's easier?

Friend: Exactly.

Director: How many people who trust in what others want are actually happy?

Friend: Exactly none.

Director: But many people trust this way?

Friend: All too many.

Director: You'd think they'd talk to one another, compare notes, figure out what's wrong.

Friend: It's funny but they can't trust others enough to do that.

Director: They trust something as important as happiness to what others want but aren't willing to trust others enough to open up and talk about their experience in this trust? Why?

Friend: I suspect it's because they already know deep down inside something of the truth about their happiness and don't like to hear it from someone else.

Director: Then how will they ever attain happiness?

Friend: Unless they start by facing the truth? They won't.

74. HAPPINESS 2 (SCIENTIST)

Director: So you believe there are different types of people? In other words, we're not all the same?

Scientist: We're far from being all the same.

Director: What's the most basic way in which we differ?

Scientist: Responsibility.

Director: Can you say more?

Scientist: Some of us think that we ourselves are responsible for our own happiness, while others think that others are responsible for it.

Director: How can someone else be responsible for our own happiness?

Scientist: In truth? He can't.

Director: But what if this person treats us terribly? Wouldn't that affect our happiness?

Scientist: Yes, of course. But it's our responsibility either to get the person to stop treating us terribly or to get away from that person.

Director: And that would make us happy?

Scientist: It would be a start.

Director: Would it be a start for everyone, or only for certain types of people?

Scientist: I think it would be a start for everyone.

Director: So we're really not all that different?

Scientist: Well, in a sense.

Director: But in the sense of responsibility, we're different?

Scientist: Very different.

Director: So let me see if I understand. While getting away from someone who treats us terribly is a start, the type of person we are as concerns responsibility will determine what we do with this start?

Scientist: Precisely.

Director: Those who take responsibility for their own happiness will strike out and search for this happiness?

Scientist: Yes.

Director: And then they'll do what they need to do to secure it?

Scientist: Certainly.

Director: But the others, those who don't take responsibility for their happiness — what will they do?

Scientist: Nothing.

Director: Nothing? But why?

Scientist: Because they expect that happiness will come to them.

Director: Just like that? As if by luck?

Scientist: That's right.

Director: So the difference is this — some will work for their happiness while others will rely on luck?

Scientist: Yes, I think that's fair to say.

Director: But what does it mean to work for happiness?

Scientist: What do you mean? You just work for it.

Director: So if having a new car would make me happy, I must work for the new car?

Scientist: Well, I suppose. But that's not the sort of happiness I'm talking about.

Director: What kind are you talking about?

Scientist: The kind that comes from human interaction.

Director: We have to work for the kind of interactions we want?

Scientist: Yes.

Director: But what if we're lucky? What if we get the kind we want without effort? Do you think that's possible? And if it's possible, is it to be preferred?

Scientist: No, I don't think it's possible. But even if it were, I, for one, would always choose to work for what I want — because work is infinitely more reliable than luck.

75. Happiness 3 (Artist)

Artist: The truth is that we all depend on others for our happiness.

Director: How so?

Artist: Look at it this way. Would you be happy without the ones you love?

Director: You're asking a terrible question, Artist.

Artist: Why is it terrible?

Director: Because you're trying corner me into saying something that would seem terrible.

Artist: Well?

Director: Let me ask you this. Do you love me as a friend?

Artist: Of course I do.

Director: If I were dying and I told you not to be sad when I'm gone, to be as happy as you can be, and to do this in memory of me — would you think that bad?

Artist: Of course not.

Director: And isn't that how all people who truly love you would approach the matter? Wouldn't they all wish you to be happy?

Artist: Yes, but wishing me to be happy and my being happy are two different things.

Director: And that's because you depend on these people for your happiness?

Artist: Yes.

Director: How do you depend on them?

Artist: What do you mean? They just make me happy when I'm around them.

Director: And I'm among those who make you happy?

Artist: Yes, of course.

Director: What is it about me that makes you happy?

Artist: You tell the truth.

Director: Truth makes you happy?

Artist: Yes.

Director: What about your art?

Artist: What about it?

Director: Do you tell the truth in your art?

Artist: I try to.

Director: And when you succeed, how do you feel? Happy?

Artist: I do.

Director: Does anyone help you when it comes to your art, or are you on your own?

Artist: I'm on my own.

Director: So it's possible for you to be happy on your own?

Artist: I guess. But I can't always be at work. No one can.

Director: And when you're not working, you depend on others for your happiness?

Artist: Yes, of course.

Director: Is what you depend on in them the truth? After all, you said truth makes you happy.

Artist: Yes, the truth of those I love is what I depend on.

Director: And what about your own truth?

Artist: What about it?

Director: Does it only come out in your art, or does it come out with those you love?

Artist: It comes out with those I love.

Director: So as far as your happiness goes, you'd never depend on someone who doesn't allow your truth to come out?

Artist: No, why would I?

Director: I don't know. But let me ask you this. Is it enough for your truth to come out with those you love, or must it also be appreciated?

Artist: It must be appreciated.

Director: Then may you always have with you those you love who appreciate your truth. And if the day should come when they're gone, then do all you can do to find your happiness again, for your own sake, and in memory of them.

76. Truth 2 (Friend)

Friend: You have to like yourself?

Director: What? Don't you think that's good advice?

Friend: It's just a bit too simple, don't you think?

Director: Sometimes the simplest advice is the best advice.

Friend: Sometimes.

Director: But even if it's not the best advice, isn't it at least good? I mean, can you be happy if you don't like yourself?

Friend: I suppose not.

Director: Then why do you think it isn't good advice to give?

Friend: Because it's hard to like yourself.

Director: What's hard about it?

Friend: We're complex beings.

Director: All of us? Or are some of us simple?

Friend: Some of us are simple.

Director: But the people you care about aren't?

Friend: No, they're not.

Director: Does that mean the people you care about sometimes don't like themselves?

Friend: Yes.

Director: Well, why wouldn't you prefer the simple people then, if what we seem to be implying is true and it's easy for them to like themselves?

Friend: Because I can't relate to them.

Director: Would you like people to not like themselves at times just so you can relate?

Friend: No, of course not. I wish we could all just like ourselves all the time.

Director: Would that mean we'd all be simple?

Friend: Yes, I guess it would.

Director: But I get the feeling that you'd really rather not be simple yourself.

Friend: Not being simple shows that you're self-critical.

Director: You mean it shows that you seek knowledge of yourself?

Friend: Yes.

Director: But can't someone who's simple have knowledge of himself?

Friend: I suppose.

Director: So it's not about knowledge? It's about being different?

Friend: What do you mean?

Director: Look at it this way. Are many people simple?

Friend: Well, maybe not many.

Director: And what about the complex people? Are there many of them?

Friend: I think most people are complex.

Director: But a few are very complex?

Friend: Yes, very.

Director: So there are three types of people? The simple, the complex, and the very complex?

Friend: Yes, I think we can say those are the three basic types.

Director: And what about the two of us? What are we?

Friend: I think we're among the most complex.

Director: Is it an honor to be among the most complex?

Friend: It can be — but only if you learn to appreciate your complexity, your truth, for what it is.

Director: And if you don't?

Friend: Then you'll never have the chance to learn to like yourself for what you really are.

77. HAPPINESS 4 (FRIEND)

Friend: I think we, as complex beings, very complex beings, are happy only rarely.

Director: The greater the complexity the more rare the happiness?

Friend: Yes.

Director: Then I'll pose the hard question, Friend. Should we strive to make ourselves simple in order to maximize our happiness? Or should we maintain our complexity despite our lack of happiness. In other words, what's good about complexity?

Friend: Complexity is a sign of sophistication.

Director: And what is sophistication?

Friend: What do you mean? Sophistication is... sophistication!

Director: And sophistication is more important than happiness?

Friend: Well, I don't know that I'd say that.

Director: Is sophistication a kind of knowledge?

Friend: Yes, it is.

Director: Knowledge of how things work and how to act?

Friend: That's sophistication, yes.

Director: Then sophistication seems to be a very good thing.

Friend: It does.

Director: But when you know how to act, do you know why you're acting that way?

Friend: What do you mean? You act that way because that's how things work.

Director: So there's a sort of inevitability in all sophistication?

Friend: Yes, I think that's true.

Director: You say to yourself, this is how things work, so I will act accordingly?

Friend: You do.

Director: And you take pride in the fact that you know how things work?

Friend: Yes.

Director: And you take pride because the less complex beings aren't as sophisticated?

Friend: Correct.

Director: So your sophistication is a distinguishing factor. Only the few are sophisticated.

Friend: Don't you think that's true?

Director: Let's assume it is. What happens to those who aren't sophisticated?

Friend: They make mistakes.

Director: And bad things happen to them when they do?

Friend: There's no doubt about that.

Director: So sophistication can be seen as a sort of prudence?

Friend: Yes, I suppose it can.

Director: Now, when people aren't prudent, and bad things happen, can they be happy?

Friend: No one is happy when bad things happen.

Director: But when people are in fact prudent, and good things happen, are they happy?

Friend: Of course.

Director: So can we say that sophistication, to the extent it involves prudence, can be a means toward happiness?

Friend: We can.

Director: But we said that complexity is a sign of sophistication.

Friend: We did.

Director: And we said the greater the complexity the more rare the happiness.

Friend: True.

Director: Then where does that leave us? How can we maintain that sophistication can be a means toward happiness if sophistication involves complexity, and happiness and complexity are opposed?

Friend: Maybe sophistication doesn't always involve complexity?

Director: You mean the simple might at times be a sign of sophistication?

Friend: Yes. But I don't like what this means.

Director: What does it mean?

Friend: That sophistication isn't as simple as it seems.

78. METHOD 2 (*ARTIST*)

Director: What method do you employ when you depict the truth?

Artist: Well, I don't just state it out-and-out.

Director: But if you don't just state it out-and-out won't some people think you don't know the truth?

Artist: That's true. But I don't care.

Director: Who will know that you know the truth?

Artist: The people who are capable of putting two and two together to make four.

Director: So you put part of the truth here and part of the truth there and don't add it up?

Artist: Yes.

Director: Why? Is that just some perversity on your part?

Artist: No. I'm creating for a sophisticated audience, the kind that doesn't need me to tell it that two plus two is four.

Director: So you only give the audience the bare essentials of what it needs?

Artist: Yes.

Director: But can't you be generous at times? Can't you tell them, for instance, that the cube of three is twenty-seven?

Artist: No. Why would I?

Director: Because you don't want them to miss the point you're making.

Artist: If they can't multiply three by three by three, then they don't deserve to get the point I'm making.

Director: Are you saying certain people can't handle certain truths?

Artist: Yes, and anyone who thinks otherwise is a fool.

Director: But the sophisticated, the ones you create for, they can handle all your truths?

Artist: Yes.

Director: And when the sophisticated figure these truths out, how do they feel?

Artist: They feel satisfied.

Director: But they wouldn't have that satisfaction if you just declared the truth out-and-out?

Artist: No, they wouldn't.

Director: Why not?

Artist: The truth wouldn't be in its proper place.

Director: Truth has a proper place?

Artist: Of course it does. What good does it do to go shouting out the number four when it's possible to place two beautiful twos discretely in the work?

Director: So it's about not hollering the answer?

Artist: Right. All crass artwork hollers. The artists seem to think if only they keep on shouting the answer someone will hear. Well, everyone hears — and these artists get the audience they deserve.

Director: Do I detect a touch of bitterness?

Artist: No, I'm just telling you how it is.

Director: Then tell me, Artist. What's your ideal audience? Can you say more than that they're sophisticated?

Artist: They're people who appreciate the delicacy of my work, the way I carefully present truths. They appreciate how I don't coat these truths with a gloss of gratuitous interpretation, how I don't draw for them the conclusions they need to draw on their own.

Director: Why do they need to draw them on their own?

Artist: Because that's the only way anyone ever really comes to know the truth.

Director: I don't know, Artist. Don't you think that sometimes we need to hear the conclusion in so many words? I mean, can't knowing that conclusion be like knowing your destination without knowing how to get there? You must work to figure out your route. And then you must work to travel that route. And in traveling it all the way that's how you really come to know. No?

Artist: Sure, Director. But who says I'm offering up a single destination?

79. METHOD 3 (FRIEND)

Friend: Satisfaction runs deeper than happiness.

Director: If that's true, isn't it very important to be able to obtain satisfaction?

Friend: Yes, of course.

Director: And if we want to obtain satisfaction in more than a haphazard way, won't we need a method for obtaining it?

Friend: Well, yes.

Director: And if we want to find the method for obtaining something, don't we have to know what that something is?

Friend: We do.

Director: Then tell me, Friend. What is satisfaction?

Friend: It's just... feeling satisfied.

Director: And is feeling satisfied always a good feeling?

Friend: It is.

Director: Can you be satisfied when you take revenge?

Friend: Yes, I guess.

Director: And is the satisfaction from revenge a good feeling?

Friend: Well, it's a feeling alright.

Director: A feeling you'd like to have?

Friend: Yes, at times.

Director: But you don't want to say it's a good feeling?

Friend: How can we say revenge is good?

Director: Then how can we say satisfaction is always good?

Friend: I guess we can't.

Director: But we still want satisfaction even though we don't think it's simply good?

Friend: We do. And that's a problem.

Director: Yes. And there's another problem. If we don't know what satisfaction is, aside from it being a feeling that's not simply good, how can we ever hope to arrive at the method for obtaining it?

Friend: I think there's a way.

Director: What way?

Friend: Look at science and its method. Does it always know what it finds? Doesn't it just sometimes find it?

Director: So we can find the way to satisfaction even though we don't know what satisfaction is?

Friend: Yes.

Director: But even if we find it, how will we know we found it?

Friend: We'll just feel it.

Director: So we'll devise a method for coming to feel a certain way. And we won't know what this feeling really is. We won't even know whether it's good or bad. We'll just know that we want it.

Friend: Yes.

Director: Should we do that with all things, Friend?

Friend: You mean devise methods for whatever we want, regardless of what it is?

Director: Yes. What do you think?

Friend: Well, some things we know are bad. So we shouldn't devise methods for obtaining them.

Director: And for the things we know are good, we should definitely devise methods for obtaining them?

Friend: Definitely.

Director: If you have yet to devise a method for something you know is good, does it make sense to spend time devising a method for something you're not sure is good?

Friend: No, I guess it doesn't. But you know what that means, don't you?

Director: Tell me.

Friend: We urgently need to prove that satisfaction is good.

80. Madness 2 (Scientist)

Scientist: The greatest madness? I don't think there's only one.

Director: How many are there?

Scientist: At least three — thirst for revenge, certain types of love, and trusting to luck.

Director: Is there a theme common to them all?

Scientist: Yes, they all induce madness by disrupting reason.

Director: Well, let's see. If I'm thirsting for revenge, wouldn't I use my reason to plot?

Scientist: Yes, that's true. But when you're truly thirsting for revenge you're blind to all other considerations.

Director: You become a monomaniac for revenge?

Scientist: Yes, and narrowing your vision down to only one thing amounts to disengaging your reason as concerns all the other things in life.

Director: I see. The certain types of love you had in mind, are they a sort of monomania?

Scientist: They certainly are.

Director: So if you're in love in a certain way, your monomania won't leave room for anything else?

Scientist: Yes, that's true.

Director: And what about trusting to luck?

Scientist: You wouldn't think it's possible, but people can be monomaniacs concerning luck.

Director: Why wouldn't it seem possible?

Scientist: Because most people think of trusting to luck as being carefree. But that's not how it is for those who truly trust to luck.

Director: How is it for them?

Scientist: Intense. They look to every chance event as a sign and they wildly try to interpret that sign.

Director: Is intensity also present in those who love in certain ways and those who thirst for revenge?

Scientist: Yes, it is.

Director: So intensity really is the common theme?

Scientist: I suppose so.

Director: But isn't intensity sometimes good? Or does it always amount to madness?

Scientist: No, sometimes it's good.

Director: What distinguishes good intensity from madness? Is it a question of degree?

Scientist: No, I don't think it is. A scientist might be intensely focused on a problem, but that wouldn't make him mad.

Director: Not even if he lets that intensity consume him?

Scientist: Well, you might have a point.

Director: So that's the idea — don't let your intensity consume you, don't let it make you mad?

Scientist: Yes, I think it is.

Director: How do you stop intensity from consuming you?

Scientist: By having a sense of irony about yourself.

Director: What do you mean by that?

Scientist: You can't take yourself too seriously.

Director: And how do you come to not take yourself too seriously, to have what we're calling a sense of irony? I mean, are certain people just born with a sense of irony? Or do they develop it?

Scientist: Oh, they develop it — usually when they're on the verge of being consumed.

81. MADNESS 3 (FRIEND)

Friend: To be consumed by madness? I think it can be a good thing.

Director: How so?

Friend: It can help you to see things in a new light.

Director: But what if it isn't a good light?

Friend: Well, maybe that's the test.

Director: The test?

Friend: Yes. If you emerge from madness and see things in a good light, you're... you're... a good person.

Director: A good person?

Friend: Yes. And if you emerge from madness and see things in a bad light, you're a bad person.

Director: What makes a good light good and a bad light bad?

Friend: It all has to do with seeing things as they are.

Director: Including yourself?

Friend: Yes, especially yourself.

Director: How do you know you're seeing things as they are?

Friend: There will be a sort of serendipity in your life.

Director: You mean you'll have good luck?

Friend: Yes.

Director: I don't understand. What does luck have to do with seeing things as they are, with being a good person?

Friend: It's karma. Karma requires good acts, and you can't act well if you can't see well.

Director: But if you see well you don't necessarily act well — or do you?

Friend: You're asking if there's a sort of inevitability about all of it? If vision is the only thing that really counts?

Director: Is it?

Friend: I think it is.

Director: So if you see well, you act well. And if you act well, you build up good karma. And if you build up good karma, then good things will happen to you.

Friend: Exactly.

Director: Then tell me this. When do you see better? When you've never been mad yet see things in a good light, or when you have been mad but have emerged from the madness and see things in a good light?

Friend: I think you see better for having been mad.

Director: Why?

Friend: Because you've seen the limits of things — gone beyond them, in fact.

Director: And in order to know things you need to have seen their limits?

Friend: Yes.

Director: But how do you know that the limits you saw while mad are truly the limits and not just imagined limits?

Friend: There's only one way to know.

Director: To test those limits once you emerge from madness?

Friend: Yes.

Director: But if you're testing limits, pushing them yourself, isn't there a risk you'll go mad once more?

Friend: What can I say? Life is a risk.

Director: But the risk always seems better with karma on your side?

Friend: Everything seems better with karma on your side.

Director: Then let's be very sure we see things for what they are.

82. DOUBT 1 (SCIENTIST)

Scientist: The only way to see things for what they are? Doubt.

Director: I don't understand.

Scientist: We must doubt then prove.

Director: So we can take nothing for granted?

Scientist: That's right.

Director: And once we've proved, we know?

Scientist: Yes.

Director: And we see by means of our knowledge?

Scientist: Of course.

Director: What's the opposite of knowledge?

Scientist: Ignorance.

Director: Are we blind when we're ignorant?

Scientist: Certainly.

Director: Is there an intermediate stage between knowledge and ignorance?

Scientist: Yes, that would be belief.

Director: When you believe, you're not blind, but you don't see as clearly as when you know?

Scientist: Well, it depends on whether what you believe is true or not.

Director: But either way, when you believe, do you think you know?

Scientist: Not necessarily. You can believe something while knowing you don't know.

Director: But if you believe something and think your belief amounts to knowledge?

Scientist: Then you're as blind as the ignorant — and maybe worse.

Director: And maybe worse?

Scientist: An ignorant man can know he's ignorant. So in a sense he knows himself. But someone who believes, but thinks he knows, doesn't know himself.

Director: Knowing yourself is seeing yourself?

Scientist: Yes.

Director: So the ignorant aren't necessarily completely blind?

Scientist: I suppose that's true, in a sense.

Director: But in order to gain in knowledge the ignorant must push back on their ignorance with doubt?

Scientist: Well, no. If we're ignorant about something, there's nothing to doubt.

Director: We have to believe in order to doubt?

Scientist: Yes, though we can doubt what others believe.

Director: And what about the things we know? Do we have to doubt them?

Scientist: No, we know what we know.

Director: But what if we only believe we know?

Scientist: Then we have to doubt.

Director: But why would we doubt if we think we know?

Scientist: You have a point. We wouldn't.

Director: So we must be given reason to doubt?

Scientist: Yes.

Director: Who can give reason to doubt to the ones who believe they know?

Scientist: Anyone who doesn't believe what they believe.

Director: But what if someone knows what the others only believe they know?

Scientific: Then it falls to him to give them his proof.

83. Doubt 2 (Artist)

Artist: Should an artist doubt his own work? No, he needs to have confidence in it.

Director: What happens if he lacks confidence in his work?

Artist: The work reflects the doubt.

Director: How?

Artist: It's hard to explain. All I can say is that everything doesn't hold together the way it should.

Director: You mean it lacks a sort of consistency?

Artist: Yes, I think that's fair to say. When an artist doubts his work he makes many false starts and doesn't correct them.

Director: Why doesn't he correct them?

Artist: He doesn't know how.

Director: But he knows the false starts make for inconsistency?

Artist: Yes, at some level.

Director: Then if he knows he's making bad art, why keep making it?

Artist: Because he wants to be an artist and this is the only way he knows how.

Director: So he makes just any old sort of inconsistent art in the belief that that will make him an artist?

Artist: Crazy, isn't it?

Director: But if he has confidence in his art? Is it a different story then?

Artist: Yes. The art will be better, more consistent.

Director: Because his confidence permeates the work?

Artist: Yes.

Director: But what if it's unwarranted confidence?

Artist: What do you mean?

Director: Well, let me ask you. What makes confidence warranted when it comes to art?

Artist: Knowledge. What else?

Director: So is it the case that some artists know and some artists merely believe they know?

Artist: It is.

Director: But confidence permeates the works of both types of artist?

Artist: I'm afraid so.

Director: And are many people taken by the confidence of those who don't know?

Artist: Yes, a great many.

Director: Why?

Artist: Because they don't know either.

Director: Will these people ever be taken by the confidence of those who know?

Artist: Not if it goes against what they think they know.

Director: But can't an artist cause them to question what they think they know?

Artist: Yes, but people don't question as often as you and I might like.

Director: Indeed. Now tell me, Artist. What sort of artist are you?

Artist: Me? I'm the sort that only doubts before I begin my work.

Director: And you only begin when you're sure you know?

Artist: That's right.

Director: But what do you do if you come to doubt while you're working?

Artist: I scrap my work, set to learn what I need to know, then start all over again.

Director: And if you learn and then doubt, and learn and then doubt?

Artist: Then patience is the only thing keeping me from making bad art.

84. Victory 1 (Artist)

Artist: Victory? Victory is being recognized.

Director: Recognized for what?

Artist: Recognized for what you know.

Director: And for an artist that recognition comes through his work?

Artist: Of course.

Director: Because the knowledge of the artist is reflected in his work?

Artist: Yes.

Director: But what if someone recognizes the knowledge of the artist in the artist himself, and not in his work? Is that a sort of victory?

Artist: I suppose.

Director: But artists find it sweeter to be recognized in their work?

Artist: They do.

Director: Why?

Artist: Their work is an accomplishment.

Director: And having knowledge itself isn't?

Artist: Well, no. It is. But it's not the same.

Director: Why not?

Artist: Because many people can see your work. But only a few people can know you personally.

Director: But can't you gain a reputation for knowledge, a reputation that would travel far and wide?

Artist: Reputations can be sullied. A great work of art can't.

Director: How is a reputation sullied?

Artist: People make things up about you.

Director: You mean they say bad things?

Artist: Yes.

Director: But can't people say bad things about your great work of art?

Artist: That's true. But anyone with eyes to see can see that it's a great work of art, regardless of what anyone else might say.

Director: And you want to be recognized by those who have eyes to see?

Artist: Of course.

Director: But if you don't come into direct contact with these people with eyes to see, how do you know they exist?

Artist: What do you mean? There are always people with eyes to see.

Director: Are there? I don't know that. What if those with eyes to see are a dying breed? What if your great work of art goes forward in time with no one to see it, to really see it for the wonderful thing it is?

Artist: You really believe that's possible?

Director: I do.

Artist: Then what can I do?

Director: You have to craft your work of art in such a way that it teaches people to see it for what it is.

Artist: Teach people to see? How do I do that?

Director: I'm sorry, Artist. I wish I could help you. But I'm not an artist. And so I don't know how to do what needs to be done.

Artist: So you're just going to tell me I need to do something that seems impossible and then offer no assistance?

Director: I'm just telling you how it seems to me. And I'm telling you that if you want to guarantee victory, this is what you must do. You must find a way.

85. VICTORY 2 (*SCIENTIST*)

Director: What's the ultimate victory as concerns science?

Scientist: The ultimate victory? I don't know that there's an ultimate victory.

Director: You mean it's not to know everything?

Scientist: I have my doubts about that as a goal.

Director: Why?

Scientist: Because every time we learn more, it seems there's more for us to learn.

Director: So we know less as we know more?

Scientist: Yes.

Director: Then why know more?

Scientist: Because we don't literally know less.

Director: We know more but we know that there's always more to learn?

Scientist: Precisely.

Director: So our knowledge, as a percentage of all there is to know, goes down as our horizons expand?

Scientist: That's a fine way of putting it.

Director: But maybe a time will come when each new discovery won't bring us to more unexplored territory.

Scientist: You mean our percentage of knowledge against the whole actually starts to increase?

Director: Yes. And if it keeps increasing, might it not reach one hundred percent?

Scientist: That seems like a dream, Director.

Director: But is it possible?

Scientist: Strictly speaking? I suppose there's no reason why it couldn't be possible.

Director: So there's the victory of science.

Scientist: But then science will have put itself out of business. What need for science if everything is known?

Director: Then maybe science gets into a new line of business.

Scientist: And what would that be?

Director: Creating the unknown.

Scientist: So science creates and then seeks to know what it has created?

Director: Yes.

Scientist: Then what's the ultimate victory of that?

Director: Smaller victories, friend. No ultimate victory. Each new creation is a victory. Each act of coming to know what such creations mean is a victory.

Scientist: Then let me ask you this. What happens when we run out of things to create and know?

Director: Then it seems science is truly out of business. Or can you think of something else for science to do?

Scientist: I'm at a loss.

Director: Well, don't worry, Scientist. I think we're a long way off from science running out of things to do.

Scientist: But it's disconcerting to think that science will come to an end even if that end is a long way off.

Director: Then we need to think what human activity can replace science when the time comes.

Scientist: I don't even know how to begin to think about that.

Director: Then maybe that's a task for science to start in earnest on today. It must study itself to know what it is, what it means to people, what role it plays in their lives. Then it must determine how it can be replaced. Can you imagine? Science completing its task and creating its own replacement? Wouldn't that be the greatest of victories, the greatest of all?

86. VICTORY 3 (*FRIEND*)

Friend: What do I think victory is? Winning.

Director: Winning?

Friend: Sure. You know. Beating the competition.

Director: There can be no victory without competition?

Friend: None.

Director: But what if you compete with yourself?

Friend: Oh, that's just nonsense. No one really competes with himself.

Director: Then what are people talking about when they talk about competing with yourself?

Friend: They're talking about not focusing on the competition. Sometimes focusing there can distract you from doing what you need to do to win. So you compete with yourself for a while, as they say.

Director: But who is this competition that you don't compete against, as they say?

Friend: It doesn't really matter.

Director: So if I'm an artist, I can, for instance, compete against other artists or I can compete against scientists?

Friend: Sure.

Director: Well, I can understand how an artist might compete against other artists. He would try to create better works than the others. But how does an artist compete against scientists?

Friend: He tries to create works of art that are better than whatever it is that the scientists come up with.

Director: So if scientists come up with knowledge, we're saying the competition is between knowledge and art?

Friend: Yes.

Director: But how can we tell who wins?

Friend: People vote.

Director: What, by means of a ballot?

Friend: No, they vote with time, their time. They simply have to decide what to spend time on — the work of art or the scientific knowledge.

Director: And victory goes to the one who wins the judge's time?

Friend: Exactly.

Director: I wonder if this ever happens.

Friend: What?

Director: Someone spends more time with the work of art, for example, but when asked, says that the scientific knowledge is more important.

Friend: Oh, I think that sort of thing happens all the time.

Director: Then who wins? The artist or the scientist?

Friend: They both win — but one has the formal victory while the other has the actual victory.

Director: If you were competing, which would you rather have?

Friend: The actual victory, of course.

Director: What do you get with an actual victory?

Friend: You get satisfaction.

Director: And what do you get if you get the formal victory?

Friend: Inflated pride.

Director: And the way to check that pride is to have the victor look at what the judges are actually doing with their time?

Friend: No better way.

Director: But what if those with the formal victory think judges don't spend time with their knowledge, or art, or whatever because it's beyond them, over their heads?

Friend: Well, they might be right. And if they are, they either learn to aim lower or rest satisfied with what they've got.

87. Nuance (Scientist)

Scientist: What's over the heads of many people? An appreciation for nuance, for subtlety.

Director: Why do you think that is?

Scientist: Two reasons. One, some people just aren't as refined as others.

Director: Is that to say their senses just aren't as good?

Scientist: Yes.

Director: What's the other reason?

Scientist: They lack patience.

Director: Patience?

Scientist: Yes. If you're in a great big hurry, you'll never pick up on the nuances of a thing.

Director: You mean like the nuances of a bottle of wine?

Scientist: Sure. If you guzzle the wine down, you'll never notice let alone appreciate its complexity.

Director: But those who both notice and appreciate the complexity, aren't they sometimes referred to as snobs?

Scientist: They are, but often wrongly so.

Director: Why wrongly so?

Scientist: What is a snob?

Director: Someone who thinks he's better than others?

Scientist: Yes. Now, just because someone can appreciate complexity, subtlety — does that necessarily make him think he's better than others who can't?

Director: Better at appreciating subtleties and complexities, yes.

Scientist: Yes, of course. But what about being better simply?

Director: Better simply?

Scientist: Better as a human being.

Director: Human beings do more than taste wine.

Scientist: Precisely.

Director: And those who know this fact, and know it very well, aren't snobs?

Scientist: That's right.

Director: I see. But what if we're talking about picking up on the nuances of something that's much more important than wine?

Scientist: Like what?

Director: What would you say is the most important thing in life?

Scientist: The most important? I'm not sure. But I can tell you what's among the most important — our interactions with others.

Director: Do those interactions sometimes involve an appreciation of nuance?

Scientist: I'd say they often do.

Director: And some can appreciate the nuances of the interactions better than others?

Scientist: Yes.

Director: Would you say that good things come of appreciating these nuances?

Scientist: I would.

Director: So some people have more good things in their lives than others?

Scientist: I suppose.

Director: All because they can and do appreciate nuance?

Scientist: Well, I don't think it's that simple.

Director: Why not?

Scientist: You can have good things in your life for reasons other than appreciating nuance.

Director: Then let's be sure we don't let our appreciation for the finer things blind us to those reasons, the reasons that deal with things that are of a nature much more obvious, and much more coarse.

88. Detail (Artist)

Artist: Is it possible for a work of art to be too detailed? I suppose.

Director: What would make it so?

Artist: When the details detract from the overall meaning.

Director: How would they do that?

Artist: They'd put the focus on the trees to the point where the audience can't see the forest.

Director: But is that really possible?

Artist: What do you mean?

Director: Can't the audience always step back and catch sight of the forest?

Artist: Well, it depends on the audience. Some audiences won't see unless they're told what to see.

Director: Are you saying that if all an artist shows are leaves, some audiences won't know enough to step back and see that all these leaves must be on or have come from trees?

Artist: Yes. But there are others who can step back and see the trees, and then take another step back and see the forest.

Director: All from the leaves?

Artist: All from the leaves.

Director: But how would they know the leaves are on a tree that's in a forest and not, say, in a city park?

Artist: The artist would have to make it clear somehow.

Director: I see. Then tell me. If an artist paints a thousand leaves and then mentions that the tree is in a forest, is his work any less detailed for having mentioned where the tree is?

Artist: Of course not. I'd say it's even more detailed for giving the location.

Director: And the location of the tree, is that part of the overall meaning of the work?

Artist: Certainly.

Director: Would that meaning be affected even if the artist were to paint a million more leaves on top of the thousand he's already painted?

Artist: No, it wouldn't affect it at all. The meaning is the meaning.

Director: Now, just to be clear — the leaves in our metaphor are the details?

Artist: Yes.

Director: And if the artist went further and depicted the veins on the leaves? That would be even more detail?

Artist: That would be a great deal of detail.

Director: But with all those veins and leaves, if he mentions that the tree is in a city park, and that information is part of the meaning, the detail of veins and leaves in no way detracts from the meaning?

Artist: Right.

Director: So does it make sense to say that a work of art can be too detailed?

Artist: It doesn't seem that it does.

Director: Then why do you think someone might be inclined to say that works of art can in fact be too detailed?

Artist: Because artists focused on the veins in the leaves of a tree often don't pay much attention to the forest or city in which the tree is found.

Director: Detail can blind artists to the larger picture?

Artist: Absolutely.

Director: So in your opinion it's best if the artist can take the comprehensive view?

Artist: Of course. And when he has, he can decide simply to mention that the tree is in a city park, if that's where the tree really is, or he can say nothing and just start depicting the city itself.

89. UNDERSTANDING (FRIEND)

Director: What is understanding?

Friend: Why do you ask? Are you trying to understand understanding?

Director: You're a funny one, Friend. If I say yes, then I'm asking about something I already know. So I think it's best to say I don't know if that's what I'm trying to do. I need to know what understanding is before I can answer your question

Friend: Well, now you're making me wonder. Is knowing the same as understanding?

Director: How can you expect me to answer that if I don't know what understanding is?

Friend: Do you at least know what knowing is?

Director: I admit I could use a little help there, too.

Friend: You seem rather helpless, Director.

Director: However that may be, what can we say about knowing and understanding?

Friend: Ah, that's a more reasonable question. Let's say they're the same thing and see where that takes us.

Director: Can you give me an example that shows they're the same?

Friend: Sure. You know two plus two equals four. You understand that two plus two equals four.

Director: Hmm. I see. How about this for a different example? You understand why someone did something. You know why someone did something.

Friend: Yes, it's the same thing in either case. Here's another. You know the English language. You understand the English language.

Director: Since you brought up language, why do you think our language has two different words for the same thing, if they are in fact the same thing?

Friend: Well, maybe they're not exactly the same thing.

Director: You mean there might be a shade of difference in the meanings?

Friend: Yes.

Director: So what's the difference?

Friend: Understanding suggests a good relationship.

Director: How so?

Friend: I can say you and I have a friendly understanding. But I can't say you and I have a friendly knowing.

Director: And what does this friendly understanding amount to?

Friend: Some sort of mutual agreement, at least in part.

Director: But if we both know the same things, don't we agree?

Friend: You and I might both know the same things, and even each other, but be hostile toward one another.

Director: Let me be sure I understand. If we know each other, we can still be enemies?

Friend: Yes.

Director: But if we understand one another?

Friend: Strictly speaking I suppose we can be enemies. But understanding suggests a sort of harmony. Knowing doesn't.

Director: So why would I ever want to know? Why not always understand, if understanding involves harmony?

Friend: Because knowledge is colder than understanding.

Director: And when would I want something cold?

Friend: When you're overheated.

Director: What overheats you? Too much understanding?

Friend: Yes, I think that can be part of it.

Director: So when I'm cold, I'll try to understand? And when I'm hot, I'll try to know?

Friend: Yes, give it a try and see how it works.

Director: I will, Friend. And I'll let you know how it goes.

90. Love 5 (*Friend*)

Director: Do you have to understand the person you love?

Friend: No, not necessarily. The person can be a mystery to you.

Director: And you love the mystery?

Friend: Yes.

Director: But if you love the mystery, do you really love the person?

Friend: What do you mean?

Director: Wouldn't it be the mystery itself you love, and not the person?

Friend: But the person is mysterious. That's what the person is.

Director: To you, yes. But is this person necessarily mysterious to everyone, or might there be someone who understands, someone who sees no mystery?

Friend: There might be someone like that.

Director: So it doesn't make sense to say the person is simply mysterious. Mysterious to you, yes. Not necessarily mysterious to others.

Friend: Alright, I agree.

Director: I wonder if you'll also agree that the person who sees no mystery can love.

Friend: Can love without mystery? In other words, you're asking if mystery is a necessary component of love?

Director: Yes.

Friend: Strictly speaking? I don't think it is. In fact, I think the one who understands will have a stronger love than the one who only sees mystery.

Director: Why?

Friend: Because understanding is a sort of bond.

Director: Is it a bond if it's only one way understanding, understanding on one side?

Friend: Well, it's better if there's understanding on both sides.

Director: Then the bond is strong?

Friend: Yes, of course.

Director: And the greater the understanding, the greater the bond?

Friend: Exactly.

Director: All the way up to the point of complete understanding?

Friend: To the extent that's possible, yes.

Director: Complete understanding, on both sides, would make for the perfect, indissoluble bond?

Friend: Yes.

Director: And perfect mystery on both sides would make for what?

Friend: One great big mess.

Director: And love is never a messy affair?

Friend: No, I'm not saying that. There's no such thing as perfect understanding. So there's always some room for misunderstanding, which means there's always something messy in love.

Director: But do you think that mystery is always a sort of misunderstanding?

Friend: Not necessarily. I mean, you can think someone is a mystery and know you don't understand the person. So you don't misunderstand. You just don't understand.

Director: Would you say that some of those who don't understand find mystery attractive?

Friend: Yes, of course.

Director: And in finding mystery attractive, does that mean they find not understanding attractive?

Friend: I guess they do, in a sense. But what if what they really find attractive is the prospect of coming to understand, of solving the mystery?

Director: Well, in that case I think they should be wary — because there's no guarantee that learning the secret brings love.

91. PHILOSOPHY 4 (*SCIENTIST*)

Scientist: Philosophy is the love of wisdom, correct?

Director: I think it's safe to say it is.

Scientist: Then tell me. What do you love about wisdom?

Director: What's not to love about wisdom?

Scientist: Yes, of course. But why do you love wisdom?

Director: Why does anyone?

Scientist: I think most people would love to have wisdom. But I don't know that they all love wisdom in others. And yet philosophers are supposed to love wisdom wherever it's found.

Director: Yes, that's true.

Scientist: Then here's what I'd like to know. Would a philosopher prefer to have wisdom himself or to simply admire it in others?

Director: Why can't he wish for both?

Scientist: Yes, but if he had to choose, what would he choose?

Director: Tell me, Scientist. When someone becomes wise, how does he become wise?

Scientist: What do you mean?

Director: I mean, must he become wise all on his own, or can he learn from others?

Scientist: I suppose he can learn from others.

Director: So when a philosopher admires someone who's wise, he would try to learn from this person?

Scientist: Yes, of course.

Director: Now, when we try to learn wisdom from another, what do you think we do?

Scientist: We try to make it our own.

Director: You mean we adopt and practice it?

Scientist: Yes.

Director: Well, I wonder if you see the problem I see.

Scientist: What problem is that?

Director: Suppose you admire a coat, but it's several sizes too big or several sizes too small for you. Would you wear the coat just because you admire it?

Scientist: No, of course not.

Director: What if wisdom is like a coat? Does one size fit all?

Scientist: I've often wondered about this, Director. It seems to me that one size does not fit all.

Director: But we can learn from the wise how a good coat should fit?

Scientist: Yes, we can see that it needs to be cut to size.

Director: So this means that what suits a wise man might not suit you or me?

Scientist: I agree. But where does that leave philosophy?

Director: Why would it leave philosophy anywhere different from where it leaves everybody else?

Scientist: Because not everyone loves wisdom.

Director: You mean there are people who wouldn't want to be wise?

Scientist: No, I mean there are people who don't admire the beautiful coats of others.

Director: Why do you think they don't?

Scientist: Oh, it could be any number of reasons. Jealousy is the first that comes to mind.

Director: Do you think philosophers are never jealous?

Scientist: I know they're never jealous.

Director: And why do you think that is?

Scientist: Because they're too busy trying to make a coat of their own to have any time to waste on something like that.

92. PHILOSOPHY 5 (ARTIST)

Artist: What would you say my philosophy is?

Director: What do you mean?

Artist: You know, my way of looking at things.

Director: Your way of looking at things as expressed in your art, or your way of looking at things in general?

Artist: An artist who expresses a different philosophy in his art and in his life in general isn't authentic.

Director: Can you give me an example of how that might be?

Artist: Sure. An artist might place a high value on freedom in his work but in his life he's slavish.

Director: You mean he doesn't live up to his ideal?

Artist: Yes.

Director: But what if it's more complicated than that?

Artist: How so?

Director: What if an artist works with characters, and the characters express different philosophies?

Artist: But there will be an overall philosophy.

Director: Will there? What if there isn't?

Artist: It's just chaos? Then chaos is the artistic philosophy. There's no getting around having a philosophy, Director.

Director: Well, that may be. But why did you ask me what your philosophy is? Don't you know?

Artist: I want to know if what I think it is is what others think it is.

Director: And what do you think it is?

Artist: I think my philosophy is one of questioning.

Director: You place a high value on raising questions?

Artist: Yes.

Director: I suppose I can see that in your work. So I agree.

Artist: Good. But you know what my next question is, don't you?

Director: Whether in your life in general you live up to your artistic philosophy?

Artist: Right.

Director: All I can say is how you seem to me when we're together. And when we're together we raise questions, don't we?

Artist: That's true. But I'm afraid I don't raise many questions with others when I'm not around you.

Director: Why don't you?

Artist: People don't seem well disposed toward questioning.

Director: But I do?

Artist: Of course you do.

Director: Does it make sense to raise questions with those who don't want them raised?

Artist: Well, that's the whole point of my art. Shouldn't it be the point of my life?

Director: Maybe the point of your art should be to help you find people who want to question with you, to look for answers with you — in life.

Artist: You really think that should be the point of my art?

Director: Is that such a bad point?

Artist: No, I guess it's not. But what happens if I find the people and we find the answers?

Director: You're worried you'll have to change your philosophy from questioning to answering? Don't worry, Artist. You can always question in a way that leads to the answers. And if you have trouble with that, I know lawyers who can show you how it's done.

93. Confidence 1 (*Scientist*)

Scientist: Of course it makes sense to question your way to the answer rather than to just give it at the outset.

Director: Why?

Scientist: Because when you question your way there, you build confidence.

Director: Your confidence or the confidence of those you're speaking with?

Scientist: Both.

Director: I can understand why the others might gain in confidence. You're building your case with them, after all. But why would you gain in confidence? You already know the answer.

Scientist: It always helps to reconfirm the answer step by step.

Director: Always? You scientists just reconfirm and reconfirm?

Scientist: Well, I suppose at a certain point you don't need to reconfirm any more.

Director: And that's the point at which you're fully confident of the answer?

Scientist: Yes.

Director: But, for the sake of others, you reconfirm beyond what you need, so they can learn? And there's no harm in that?

Scientist: No, no harm — good, in fact.

Director: Is this just the case when it comes to matters of science? Or can you think of something else that this procedure applies to?

Scientist: I suppose it applies to just about anything.

Director: What about questions of morality?

Scientist: You mean like what's the moral thing in a given situation, an actual situation?

Director: Yes. How does a question like that differ from a question that science might ask? In other words, why can't you just posit a hypothesis, test it, and either stick to it as a conclusion, one you can demonstrate step by step, or start all over again and form another hypothesis if necessary?

Scientist: You can't do that because life isn't a lab.

Director: You mean you only get one chance to get it right?

Scientist: Right.

Director: But in science you get many chances to get it right?

Scientist: As many as you need.

Director: How do you know when you've got it right in science?

Scientist: The facts tell you that your hypothesis is correct.

Director: And then the hypothesis becomes a principle that explains the facts?

Scientist: Yes.

Director: So a good scientist will always listen to the facts for the sake of arriving at a good principle?

Scientist: He will.

Director: And what about a good moralist? Does he always listen to the facts of a situation for the sake of arriving at a good principle?

Scientist: Of course not.

Director: Why not?

Scientist: Because a good moralist always starts out from a principle.

Director: So good moralists and good scientists proceed in the exact opposite way? One starts from principles and applies them to facts; the other starts from facts and arrives at principles?

Scientist: Yes.

Director: And is that how it should be?

Scientist: For science, yes, of course. But as for morality? I just don't see how it could be any other way.

94. Confidence 2 (Artist)

Artist: An artist without confidence is worthless.

Director: Why?

Artist: Because he'll never express his full potential.

Director: He's always holding something back?

Artist: Yes.

Director: But what's wrong with holding something in reserve? Isn't being reserved a sign of confidence?

Artist: If it is, then we need to distinguish between holding something in reserve and holding something back.

Director: What's the difference?

Artist: When you hold something in reserve you're confident because you know you can employ whatever it is whenever you want.

Director: And those who hold something back don't know that they can employ whatever it is whenever they want?

Artist: Right.

Director: Those who hold something in reserve, must they have at least at one point employed this reserve?

Artist: That makes sense. How could they know they can employ it if they never have?

Director: And isn't that the problem with those who hold something back? They've never employed it?

Artist: I think you're right.

Director: So how do we work with those who hold something back?

Artist: We have to make them feel safe, safe enough to let loose.

Director: Is all letting loose good?

Artist: No, of course not.

Director: Then how do we help the ones who hold something back know what to let loose with?

Artist: We need to know what's good to let loose with.

Director: And how do we know that?

Artist: Through our own experience.

Director: But what if someone is holding something back that neither you nor I have any experience with?

Artist: That's harder then. We might encourage him to let loose and it might not be good.

Director: Isn't it possible that it's the very fear of it not being good that keeps him in check in the first place?

Artist: I think it is. But what can we do? Tell him it'll be good even though we don't know if it will?

Director: I don't think we should lie to him.

Artist: Then what? Tell him we know he has something inside that he's holding back that may or may not be good?

Director: I think that's exactly what we tell him.

Artist: And then?

Director: We tell him we're willing to work with him.

Artist: By doing what?

Director: Slowly and gently helping him release what's inside.

Artist: And if it makes for bad art?

Director: Then he knows what he's dealing with. But if it's good? Well, then we have reason to celebrate, don't we?

95. CONFIDENCE 3 (FRIEND)

Friend: Confidence is overrated.

Director: How so?

Friend: I know lots of people who are very confident that I don't think are good.

Director: Confidence doesn't make you good?

Friend: Of course it doesn't.

Director: Then what makes you good?

Friend: Being a good person.

Director: But what does that mean?

Friend: You know. Being honest. Being kind. Being fair.

Director: But if you're honest, and kind, and fair — don't you have reason to be confident?

Friend: I'd like to think you do.

Director: What would stop such a person from being confident?

Friend: I honestly don't know.

Director: Do you think it would be better for all of us if such people were confident? Or is it better if they lack confidence?

Friend: Of course it's better if they're confident.

Director: Why?

Friend: Because then they'd be better able to exercise their virtues.

Director: You mean those who lack confidence are less honest, kind, and fair than those with the same virtues who are full of confidence?

Friend: I don't know I'd say they're less honest and so on. But having confidence gives them greater scope.

Director: You mean they're just as honest, but being confident would make their honesty reach more people?

Friend: Yes, exactly. And it's the same with their kindness and fairness.

Director: But how do they reach more people?

Friend: Their confidence allows them to get into positions that make this possible.

Director: You mean like positions of leadership?

Friend: Yes.

Director: Hmm. I'm feeling something of a terrible doubt, Friend.

Friend: Why?

Director: Do you think most leaders are less than they ought to be?

Friend: Many, if not most.

Director: And this means they're less kind, and honest, and fair than they should be?

Friend: It does.

Director: Why do you think that is?

Friend: Why aren't many leaders truly virtuous? I don't know. Why do you think they aren't?

Director: Well, here's where my doubt comes in. What if they really are truly virtuous?

Friend: What? How can that be?

Director: It can be, if they're doing the job they're asked to do well.

Friend: You're talking about a relative virtue, virtue as relative to the job they're asked to do?

Director: That's what my doubt is, Friend. What do you think?

Friend: I think it's nonsense. Virtue is virtue. It's never good to be less kind or honest or fair than you should.

Director: So it's not good for leaders with less than their full share of these things to succeed?

Friend: Of course not.

Director: Then why do so many people worship their success?

96. Fear 1 (Friend)

Friend: I think people worship the success of people who are less than good because they don't know what goes into that success.

Director: What goes into it?

Friend: Bad things.

Director: Do you think the people who worship this success are capable of doing these bad things?

Friend: Why do you say capable? You make as sound as if they're incompetent if they're not.

Director: No, of course I don't mean that. Maybe I should ask instead if these people are willing to do bad things?

Friend: That's a better question. I think the answer is no, most of them aren't.

Director: Why do you think some of those who succeed are willing to do bad things while many of their worshippers aren't?

Friend: I think it has to do with fear.

Director: Fear? Really?

Friend: Yes. The ones who succeed this way aren't afraid to do bad things.

Director: But just to be clear, not all those who do bad things succeed?

Friend: Of course not.

Director: And not all those who succeed have done bad things?

Friend: Right.

Director: Alright. Now, those who do succeed through bad things, why aren't they afraid?

Friend: They think nothing bad will happen to them as a result of their deeds.

Director: Does something bad happen to them?

Friend: For the most part? Nothing as bad as they deserve.

Director: Then they were right?

Friend: Generally speaking? I guess we have to say they were.

Director: But don't many people believe that bad things happen to people who do bad things, that karma catches up with them? Don't you believe that?

Friend: I do. But let's just say karma isn't always as good at punishment as it should be.

Director: I see. Well, tell me. Is being cruel a bad thing?

Friend: Of course.

Director: If someone who is successful is cruel, would people who worship from afar necessarily know this fact?

Friend: No.

Director: But those who work closely with the successful one would?

Friend: Yes.

Director: Then those who know about the cruelty wouldn't worship?

Friend: No, I think you're wrong. They might very well worship.

Director: I don't understand. Why worship someone who's cruel?

Friend: They wouldn't worship the person. They'd worship his success.

Director: So the only ones who'd worship the person in such a case are those who don't see what's really going on?

Friend: Right.

Director: And those who do see what's going on, and see that there's cruelty, to keep to our example — is it possible they'll be afraid of the one with success?

Friend: Yes, it's certainly possible. But I'll tell you something else they might very well be afraid of, something even worse.

Director: What's that?

Friend: Their own success.

Director: Why would they be afraid of that?

Friend: Because they think they know what it takes to succeed — and it isn't very good.

97. FEAR 2 (ARTIST)

Artist: Afraid of my own success? Of course not.

Director: And did you have to do bad things in order to enjoy the success you now have?

Artist: No, though I'm not sure everyone would agree with me about what I've done.

Director: Would you say you have to decide for yourself about that, about whether what you've done is bad or good?

Artist: We all must decide about that for ourselves.

Director: But do we all actually do so?

Artist: No, I think you have a point. We don't.

Director: Why do you think we don't?

Artist: Because we're afraid.

Director: Afraid of what?

Artist: Of what other people say.

Director: You mean if most people say something is bad, we might be afraid to say it's good?

Artist: Yes.

Director: And that's even if we only say it to ourselves?

Artist: Right. But we need to do more than say it to ourselves.

Director: We need to say it to others?

Artist: Yes, but we also need to be able to act.

Director: But we're afraid to speak and act?

Artist: You're not, Director. But most people are.

Director: So what do most people do?

Artist: They don't think or say or do anything unless they know what most people think and say and do.

Director: So they're never spontaneous? They always put out feelers first?

Artist: Yes. But sometimes they can't help it and they're spontaneous despite themselves.

Director: When does this happen?

Artist: When the pressure of the truth overcomes their fear.

Director: The pressure of the truth?

Artist: Yes. It's simply true that certain things are good or bad. If most people think they're the opposite of what they really are, it creates a tension.

Eventually, when the tension is great enough, the good or bad bursts through, spontaneously.

Director: Then if you know the truth about these things, wouldn't it be better to speak and act upon that truth deliberately rather than to say or do nothing and have things burst unexpectedly?

Artist: Yes, that would be better.

Director: So those who know the truth should get in the habit of speaking their minds and acting on what they say?

Artist: They should.

Director: But mustn't they be prudent in how they speak and act?

Artist: Of course. But it's always more prudent to speak and act deliberately than to simply let things burst.

Director: Yes, I'm inclined to agree. But I wonder what you think about something.

Artist: What?

Director: Isn't letting things burst always the way of the coward? I mean, you don't have to do anything. You just let things build and build with no effort on your part.

Artist: That's true. That's why I always speak my mind and act through my art.

Director: But what about those who have no art? What do they do?

Artist: They just speak and act in other ways.

Director: And if they just speak and act in these ways of theirs, nothing will burst?

Artist: Well, no. Sometimes speaking or acting artlessly can itself be a form of letting things burst.

Director: Then it seems we all need our art.

98. Fear 3 (Scientist)

Director: Have you ever heard it said that fear helps us know we're alive?

Scientist: I have.

Director: Do you think it's true?

Scientist: I do.

Director: So if we have no fears we might suspect we're dead?

Scientist: Yes, I suppose we might.

Director: Do you believe in the living dead?

Scientist: It's not a matter of belief. I know such people exist.

Director: You know it scientifically?

Scientist: No, not exactly.

Director: How do you know it then?

Scientist: Through the way they are when I interact with them.

Director: How does someone with no fear act? Is he violent, aggressive?

Scientist: No, not at all. He's usually very flat and mild.

Director: Flat as in no depth of soul?

Scientist: Precisely. Fear deepens the soul.

Director: I see. But why do you think the fearless, the shallow, are mild?

Scientist: They have nothing to stir them. And even if they did, they have little to be stirred.

Director: Are you saying that fear stirs us? I thought fear paralyzes.

Scientist: It depends, Director.

Director: On what?

Scientist: If you're shallow and unaccustomed to fear, a great and unexpected fear will paralyze you.

Director: But if you're deep and know fear well, and you feel great fear, you're stirred?

Scientist: Yes.

Director: So fear can be good, beyond helping you know you're alive?

Scientist: It can.

Director: Well, Scientist, if that's true then it's good news indeed. But are we sure we want to say that those who are shallow are the living dead?

Scientist: Why wouldn't we?

Director: Maybe there are times when it's good to be shallow.

Scientist: Name one.

Director: Well, how about times when you might be tempted to read too much into things?

Scientist: Do you think deep people tend to do that?

Director: More so than shallow people. Or wouldn't you agree?

Scientist: No, I suppose you're right.

Director: So maybe it's good to be deep in general but it's also good to become shallow on occasion?

Scientist: And how does someone do that?

Director: If it's true that fear deepens the soul, wouldn't the opposite hold?

Scientist: You mean if you lose your fear, you'll become more shallow?

Director: Yes. When you want to stop reading too much into things, just lose your fear. What do you think?

Scientist: I think that's easier said than done.

Director: Agreed. But it's possible?

Scientist: It's possible. But I think it's important to distinguish between people who are shallow some of the time and people who are shallow all of the time.

Director: Yes, I agree. It's very important. But, fortunately, no more clear distinction exists.

99. HOPE 3 (FRIEND)

Director: Who hopes more? The shallow or the deep person?

Friend: The deep person.

Director: Why?

Friend: The deep person has more room in his soul to contain a greater amount of hope.

Director: But, Friend, if I have a big garage does it necessarily mean I have a big car?

Friend: No, of course not.

Director: So not every deep person necessarily has more hope than someone who is shallow?

Friend: I suppose that's true.

Director: He just has a greater capacity for hope.

Friend: I agree.

Director: But this isn't to make little of the hope of shallow people.

Friend: Of course not. Hope is important to everyone who has it.

Director: Why is that?

Friend: Because hope can keep you going.

Director: And it's important to keep going.

Friend: Very important.

Director: Where are we going when we keep on going?

Friend: Ideally? Where we hope to go.

Director: So hope is about a destination?

Friend: Yes.

Director: Are some destinations good and others bad?

Friend: Of course.

Director: How do you know the difference between the two?

Friend: You know when you arrive.

Director: You mean you might be hoping against hope for many years and when you finally arrive at your destination, you might see that it's bad?

Friend: I hate to say it, but yes — that's true.

Director: But what does this mean? Is it foolish to have great, long range hopes?

Friend: No, but you need to keep checking that you're heading in the right direction along the way.

Director: How do you do that?

Friend: I think you need good friends.

Director: You share your hopes with your good friends?

Friend: Of course.

Director: But what about your deepest, most cherished hope? Do you really ever share that with anyone?

Friend: I think you should, Director.

Director: Why?

Friend: Because your friends, if they're good friends, can tell you if you're crazy in your hope.

Director: So in addition to good and bad hopes, we have crazy and sane hopes?

Friend: No doubt.

Director: And you would only encourage a friend in his sane hopes?

Friend: You're not really a friend if you encourage crazy hopes.

Director: But what makes a hope crazy?

Friend: A hope is crazy when it's unattainable.

Director: But how do we know, really know, that something is unattainable for someone else?

Friend: In certain cases you can just tell, Director.

Director: But how? How do we know that by discouraging someone in his hope we're not stifling something potentially great?

Friend: If we never see any of the many little signs of greatness along the way? We know.

100. Faith 1 (Artist)

Artist: We have to have faith in ourselves.

Director: But what does that mean? Do you mean we have to have faith that we're real?

Artist: No, not that.

Director: Do you mean we have to have faith in our special powers?

Artist: What? No, of course not.

Director: Well, what does it mean to have faith in yourself?

Artist: It means you have faith that you can do things.

Director: What kind of things?

Artist: Difficult things.

Director: But what if you can't do them? What happens to your faith?

Artist: Well, people sometimes lose faith in themselves.

Director: What happens to them then?

Artist: They often fall into despair.

Director: Faith keeps you from despair?

Artist: Absolutely.

Director: But I'm not sure I understand. If you have faith that you can do something difficult, and you try and try and try, and you just can't do it — couldn't your very faith drive you to despair?

Artist: Well, it depends on what sort of difficult thing you're talking about. Is it just very difficult or is it impossible?

Director: How would someone who has faith in himself know the difference?

Artist: You can't always tell until you try.

Director: But how do you know when you've tried enough? And when you know that, what do you do, just stop having faith in yourself as concerns the thing in question?

Artist: I don't know, Director. These are hard questions.

Director: Do you believe there's ever a time when you should stop trying?

Artist: Well, it does no good to beat your head against the wall.

Director: No, I don't imagine it does.

Artist: But you can go around the wall sometimes, and maybe even climb over it.

Director: But if you can't?

Artist: You have find another way to get past the wall. Maybe you dig under it.

Director: Maybe. But if that doesn't work and there's no other way?

Artist: Then maybe you give up.

Director: Do you just give up and do nothing else?

Artist: No, you have to try something else — something better.

Director: Better because it's not impossible for you to do?

Artist: Yes.

Director: So true faith involves knowing what's possible?

Artist: It does. Otherwise it's blind faith.

Director: Then may the knowledge of our faith be bright and clear.

101. Faith 2 (*Scientist*)

Director: Scientist, do scientists have faith?

Scientist: Of course. They're like anyone else in that respect.

Director: Yes, but do they have a faith particular to scientists?

Scientist: You mean is there a scientific faith? There is. It's a faith in progress.

Director: Progress in knowledge?

Scientist: Yes.

Director: And progress implies that things are always getting better?

Scientist: Certainly.

Director: So the more knowledge we have, the better off we are?

Scientist: Right.

Director: Do we have more knowledge now than we had, say, a hundred years ago?

Scientist: A great deal more.

Director: And are we better off now than we were before?

Scientist: In many respects, yes.

Director: But not in all respects?

Scientist: No, I don't believe we're better off in all respects.

Director: Are we worse off or are we the same?

Scientist: I think we're worse off in some respects and the same in others.

Director: What's an example of something we're worse off in?

Scientist: Manners.

Director: Are manners a function of knowledge?

Scientist: Well, you can know what good manners are.

Director: And many people today don't know what good manners are?

Scientist: Are you surprised?

Director: No, I'm not. But did they once know what good manners were?

Scientist: A hundred years ago, yes.

Director: So the people of a hundred years ago had more knowledge than we do in this respect?

Scientist: I think that's fair to say.

Director: So while we progressed in some things, we regressed in others?

Scientist: Yes.

Director: Don't you think you should do something about this?

Scientist: What's to be done?

Director: Can't you recover the lost knowledge concerning manners?

Scientist: It's not a question of recovering the knowledge. I already have it.

Director: Then can't you share it?

Scientist: And how do you suppose I'd do that?

Director: Why, just teach people what good manners are.

Scientist: Who do you think is going to want to learn?

Director: Oh, I don't know. Couldn't it be that some people with bad manners just don't know what good manners are?

Scientist: I suppose that's possible. But teaching good manners doesn't exactly further the cause of science.

Director: Your faith in progress doesn't include the progress that might be made in human interactions?

Scientist: You have a point. But it's one thing to have knowledge of what good manners are, and it's another thing entirely to live by that knowledge.

Director: Then it seems it isn't enough to teach people what you know. You must also teach them why it's best for them to live by what they can learn from you. Or is that asking too much of science, Scientist?

102. COURAGE 4 (*SCIENTIST*)

Director: What's the courage of a scientist?

Scientist: That which is involved in exploding popular misconceptions about the nature of the world.

Director: The world? I take it you also mean all things within the world and not just the world itself?

Scientist: What else?

Director: And humans are within the world?

Scientist: Certainly.

Director: What takes more courage? Exploding misconceptions about the physical world — for instance, about the bottom of the sea — or exploding misconceptions about humans?

Scientist: Humans.

Director: And what takes more courage as concerns humans? Exploding misconceptions about, for example, the physical heart, or exploding misconceptions about human interrelations?

Scientist: Human interrelations.

Director: Why do you think that is?

Scientist: Because human interrelations are often highly charged.

Director: But couldn't science help to defuse these situations?

Scientist: How do you imagine it could do that?

Director: By making clear the basis for the conflict as the first step toward resolution.

Scientist: Don't you think people know perfectly well why they have conflicts with others?

Director: I think they think they know perfectly well why they have conflicts with others. But I don't know that they always know the real reasons.

Scientist: And it's the job of science to find those reasons?

Director: Don't you think it is?

Scientist: Why would it be?

Director: Because it's the job of science to find the reasons for everything.

Scientist: Well, I suppose that's true.

Director: Isn't that the grandest view of itself for science to take?

Scientist: Of course.

Director: But some scientists might be scared at the prospect?

Scientist: True.

Director: What happens with scientists who are afraid of the true scope of science?

Scientist: They focus on things that are seemingly safe, conflict free.

Director: What's conflict free in this world?

Scientist: In truth? Nothing. Even if you study the amoeba, there's conflict.

Director: Do you think it's possible that a great aversion to conflict might make a person unfit to be a scientist?

Scientist: I do.

Director: Because it's the job of the scientist to explode misconceptions?

Scientist: Well, maybe explode is too strong a word.

Director: Still, scientists must clear up misconceptions, right?

Scientist: Right.

Director: And it takes courage to clear them up?

Scientist: Yes, it does.

Director: Then what else can we conclude but that the true scientist must be brave?

103. LEGACY 1 (SCIENTIST)

Director: So what do you want your legacy to be, Scientist?

Scientist: My legacy? My contribution to the general store of human knowledge.

Director: And anyone can make use of this knowledge?

Scientist: Yes, certainly.

Director: Anyone who is qualified or anyone in general?

Scientist: What do you mean by qualified?

Director: I mean anyone who knows enough about your area of expertise to be able to make sense of your contribution.

Scientist: Ah, but that's precisely what I've tried to avoid.

Director: You've tried to stop anyone from being able to make sense of your contribution?

Scientist: What? No. I've tried to avoid making things so complicated that you have to know much about my area of expertise in order to get the general idea of my contribution.

Director: You're a generalist?

Scientist: I like to make my work generally accessible.

Director: Because that will enhance your legacy?

Scientist: No, because I believe in the diffusion of scientific knowledge.

Director: So that means there's nothing arcane about your work?

Scientist: Well, the details of my work are only fully understood by certain specialists.

Director: So the people in general don't fully understand your work?

Scientist: No, of course not. But they get the idea.

Director: And the idea is what counts?

Scientist: Yes.

Director: So you have two legacies.

Scientist: What do you mean?

Director: You have a legacy in the general idea and you have a legacy in the particulars.

Scientist: Yes, I suppose that's fair to say.

Director: But let's suppose you could only have one legacy. Which would you choose?

Scientist: I'd choose the legacy in the particulars.

Director: Why?

Scientist: Because the general idea without the particulars amounts to nothing. But the particulars without the general idea might one day lead to a general idea.

Director: Because one of those who understand the particulars might promote the general idea that's associated with them?

Scientist: Precisely.

Director: But what if the particulars admit of more than one general idea?

Scientist: What do you mean?

Director: I mean, what if someone who understands the particulars uses them to promote a general idea different than the one you would have promoted?

Scientist: Well, if the particulars really admit of that general idea, I suppose I have no complaint.

Director: But what if that general idea runs contrary to how you see the basic import of your work?

Scientist: That wouldn't be possible.

Director: Why not?

Scientist: Because that would require a forced interpretation of the particulars.

Director: You mean forced interpretations aren't possible?

Scientist: I guess I shouldn't say they aren't possible.

Director: Then it seems you should take care in whose hands you leave your legacy.

104. Legacy 2 (Artist)

Artist: It doesn't matter in whose hands I leave my legacy. My work speaks for itself.

Director: But wouldn't you want someone to promote your work? Or will that just happen on its own?

Artist: Well, it's true that a bit of promotion doesn't hurt.

Director: As long as it properly represents your work?

Artist: Yes, you're right to point that out. That's always the problem with promotion.

Director: Do you think the only one who can promote a work the way it should be promoted is the artist himself?

Artist: No, I think it's possible for someone else to do a good job. But he has to understand the work as well as the artist himself — and sometimes even better.

Director: Now, Artist, you surprise me. You really think certain promoters might understand a work of art better than its creator?

Artist: Yes. If the promoter is himself an artist, and a greater artist than the artist who created the work, it's possible he'll know the work best.

Director: So if such an artist were charged with your legacy, you'd be pleased?

Artist: I'd be more pleased if he promoted my work during my life.

Director: Why?

Artist: Because then I'd learn from him.

Director: What do you think you'd learn?

Artist: What else? My strengths and weaknesses.

Director: And learning about them might help make you a better artist?

Artist: How else can you improve?

Director: Yes, I take your point. But tell me. When a true artist promotes your work, to whom does he promote it?

Artist: What do you mean?

Director: I mean, does he promote it to all, to any who'll listen? Or does he promote it to a select few?

Artist: Well, those who listen are likely to be few. So it's the same either way.

Director: But what if people listen but don't understand? Would you be happy to have a legacy with them?

Artist: No. If I'm to have a legacy, I want it to be among those who understand.

Director: So this promotion must happen on a personal level, to check for understanding?

Artist: Yes, it must.

Director: But we're asking much of this artist. Doesn't he have his own work to do?

Artist: He does. But you can't work all the time.

Director: So he'll promote your work when he's at leisure?

Artist: Yes.

Director: But what if he's a hard worker and leaves himself little leisure?

Artist: Then my work will get little promotion.

Director: And if little promotion, not much by way of legacy?

Artist: Not necessarily. Remember, my work speaks for itself.

Director: So all it takes is getting your work in front of those who'll appreciate it?

Artist: Yes, and, in fact, that's all an artist-promoter would do — get my work in front of the right people.

Director: And you can't know the right people unless you really know the art?

Artist: That's how it goes.

Director: But does it work the other way, too?

Artist: What do you mean?

Director: Can you really know the art if you don't know the right people? I mean, aren't people the subject of your art? And if you don't know people like the ones in the art — can you really know the art?

105. LEGACY 3 (FRIEND)

Friend: What do you think your legacy will be, Director?

Director: Being remembered by a handful of friends.

Friend: And you're satisfied with that?

Director: Why wouldn't I be?

Friend: I thought you might have greater ambitions.

Director: What, like being famous?

Friend: Sure, why not?

Director: What if I say I'm content to be famous among my friends?

Friend: But that's not really fame.

Director: Oh? I have to be famous among my enemies, too?

Friend: That's not what I meant. Real fame means being known by people you don't even know.

Director: But if I don't know them, how can they know me?

Friend: They know of you.

Director: And what does knowing of me mean? Knowing by means of hearsay?

Friend: Well, yes.

Director: Hearsay, then, is the basis of my legacy?

Friend: You're not making it sound very good.

Director: Can you make it sound good?

Friend: No, I suppose I can't. But you know what the problem is, don't you? You don't give people anything to know you by.

Director: But I give people my words and deeds.

Friend: I'm talking about the people who don't know you personally.

Director: Do you mean giving them something like a work of art?

Friend: Yes, exactly.

Director: But then the people who don't know me personally still wouldn't know me. They'd only know my work of art.

Friend: But you can be known through your art.

Director: But even if I write an autobiography, how can anyone know that what I say about myself through this art of mine is true?

Friend: You have a point.

Director: And even if what I say is true, what guarantee is there that my audience will truly come to know me through it? Do people always appreciate a work of art for what it is?

Friend: No. But then we could say that no one who's famous through a work of art can be sure that he's truly known by those with whom he's famous.

Director: Maybe that's just the nature of that kind of fame — and maybe even all of fame. But it seems it's a problem for more than just the famous.

Friend: How so?

Director: How common do you think it is to be truly known for what you are, even among those with whom you're personally acquainted?

Friend: For what you really are? It's not that common.

Director: So you'd agree that just building my little legacy among my friends, getting them to really know me, is an accomplishment?

Friend: Yes, I suppose it is.

Director: And if this legacy of mine amounts to being known by my friends, and fame does not amount to being known, known in the strict and true sense — wouldn't this legacy of mine be greater than that of fame, no matter how great that fame might be?

Friend: That seems to follow from what we've said. But somehow I don't want to agree.

Director: You'd rather not be known than known?

Friend: Why can't I be both — known by my friends and famous? Why can't you?

Director: What, so my friends can know one thing about me and strangers can think they know something else? What good comes of that?

106. Beginnings 1 (Scientist)

Director: What makes for a new beginning in science, Scientist?

Scientist: The formulation of a new question.

Director: You mean all the questions haven't already been asked?

Scientist: Of course not.

Director: But how would you know?

Scientist: Because new questions are asked every day.

Director: But does that necessarily mean that a new question will be asked tomorrow?

Scientist: Strictly speaking, no. But it seems highly likely one will.

Director: What kind of question do you think will be asked tomorrow?

Scientist: What kind?

Director: Yes. A general question, a particular question?

Scientist: Well, it's generally particular questions that tend to come up.

Director: Why?

Scientist: Because the work that scientists do suggests them.

Director: You mean if I'm working on problem X, problem Y might suggest itself to me in the course of my work?

Scientist: Precisely.

Director: And then when I'm working on problem Y, problem Z might suggest itself?

Scientist: That's how it goes.

Director: But who ever asks if we're working with the right alphabet?

Scientist: What do you mean?

Director: I mean what if problem X isn't really problem X? What if we're looking at it in the wrong way entirely? What if it's really a problem best described by a letter, or even a group of letters, a word, from an entirely different alphabet, from an entirely different language?

Scientist: That's not a question that gets asked every day.

Director: But if it were asked, wouldn't it make for a new beginning?

Scientist: If it were more than just crazy speculation? Yes.

Director: How would we know whether or not it's just crazy speculation?

Scientist: The grounds for the question would need to be articulated.

Director: And how would someone do that?

Scientist: By translating from this new language of yours.

Director: But what if there's no equivalent in our old language for the word the new language uses to describe the problem?

Scientist: Then before this new beginning can be made, people would have to learn the new language and come to understand the word in question.

Director: And that's not a matter of a day.

Scientist: No, not by any stretch of the imagination.

Director: Given that, who do you think would make the effort to learn the new language?

Scientist: The ambitious.

Director: The ambitious? Why?

Scientist: Because they want to be present at the beginning. All great beginnings involve excitement and the possibility of fame.

Director: If that's true, then why don't people ask fundamental questions and make such beginnings more often?

Scientist: Because it takes greatness even to know enough to ask a question like that.

Director: Do you think I'm great for having raised the question about scientific language?

Scientist: Ha! Of course not. For one, you have no real problem. And for another, you have no new language. It would take both to be great. But you know that.

107. BEGINNINGS 2 (*ARTIST*)

Director: Are new beginnings possible in art, Artist?

Artist: What do you mean? Are you asking whether artists are always doomed to be limited by the tradition to which they belong?

Director: Yes.

Artist: Well, almost all of them are.

Director: But new beginnings are possible?

Artist: They are.

Director: How?

Artist: The artist has to step outside the tradition.

Director: You make it sound easy.

Artist: Oh, well it's not.

Director: Why not?

Artist: In order to step outside the tradition, you first have to have understood the tradition.

Director: And understanding the tradition is hard?

Artist: I'm not just talking about taking an art history class. By understanding, I'm talking about obtaining a mastery over the tradition.

Director: How do you master tradition?

Artist: You have to have lived it.

Director: Lived it? But aren't there many different aspects to any tradition?

Artist: There are, and you have to have lived them all.

Director: And how do you do that?

Artist: You adopt, however provisionally, the point of view of each of the great artists within the tradition. And then you create from that perspective.

Director: And when you've created from all these perspectives, you'll discover your own unique perspective, your new beginning?

Artist: Yes.

Director: But what if an artist comes along and says he doesn't need to bother with tradition. He feels his perspective is unique without all that effort. He just sets to work and has his new beginning. Couldn't that be the case?

Artist: The world of art is filled with people like that. They think they're doing something new, but they're as much within the tradition as anyone.

Director: But how can that be, if they're not even aware of the tradition?

Artist: If you're not aware that you live on a planet called Earth, does that mean that you don't live on that planet?

Director: Of course not. I take your point. But now another question occurs to me.

Artist: What?

Director: Aren't there other inhabitable planets?

Artist: You mean other traditions?

Director: Yes.

Artist: Of course there are. Each has its way of looking at things.

Director: If someone is aware that there are many ways of looking at things, how does he know which way is the way for him?

Artist: I can only tell you how I know. I follow the tradition that has the most new beginnings.

Director: And in this tradition you follow, a new beginning amounts to a carrying on of the tradition, but somehow from outside the tradition?

Artist: Yes. My tradition is, in a sense, the tradition that transcends tradition.

Director: I see. But what happens to your tradition if there comes a day when there are no more great artists to make new, transcendent beginnings?

Artist: What happens to it? Nothing. And so it dies.

108. BEGINNINGS 3 (FRIEND)

Friend: Each new person we meet is a new beginning, Director.

Director: What makes the person a new beginning?

Friend: We have the chance to make a fresh impression.

Director: An impression unlike any other we've ever made?

Friend: Yes.

Director: But how is that possible?

Friend: What do you mean?

Director: Look at it this way. When an object impresses itself on something else, what happens?

Friend: Part of it comes in contact with the other thing.

Director: And this contact makes for the impression?

Friend: Yes.

Director: Well, when we make an impression on a person, what comes in contact?

Friend: All of us.

Director: So our feet come in contact with the person?

Friend: No, of course not.

Director: Our hands?

Friend: No, not usually.

Director: How about our nose?

Friend: No, not our nose.

Director: Our ears?

Friend: No.

Director: What about our eyes?

Friend: Yes, our eyes definitely make an impression.

Director: Because eyes are expressive?

Friend: Exactly.

Director: What about our mouth? Isn't it expressive in what comes out of it?

Friend: Yes, but it gets more complicated here.

Director: Why?

Friend: Because words come from what we think.

Director: And what we think can make an impression?

Friend: Yes, but sometimes we hide what we think.

Director: So our impression on another varies depending on what we hide and what we show?

Friend: Of course.

Director: Now, we said our fresh impression might be unlike any other we've ever made.

Friend: We did. And if we show more of what we think than ever before, the impression will be unique.

Director: But in order for there to be an impression, there must be contact, right?

Friend: True.

Director: When we share a thought, where is contact made?

Friend: In the thought of the other.

Director: But contact can only be made if his thought meets ours at some point, right?

Friend: Yes, that's true.

Director: And if our thought doesn't meet his, we'll make no impression at all?

Friend: Well, no. We'll definitely make an impression.

Director: But how can that be? What comes in contact to make the impression?

Friend: Sometimes the absence of contact makes the greatest impression of all.

109. KNOWING 1 (SCIENTIST)

Director: How can we ever really know something, Scientist?

Scientist: Well, if you can make it, you know it.

Director: But people can make children and they don't always know them.

Scientist: Yes, that's true. But I'm talking about making things under laboratory conditions.

Director: You've never made something in the lab and not known what it is?

Scientist: Never.

Director: Not even by accident?

Scientist: If you only make it by accident, and can't reproduce it, you haven't made it in the sense I mean.

Director: I see. Well let's suppose for argument's sake that you can make children in the lab, and that the process is reproducible. Do you know the children?

Scientist: You know them, yes. But you don't know what they'll become.

Director: What would it take to know what they'll become?

Scientist: I don't think we want to know that, Director.

Director: Why not?

Scientist: What would become of free will?

Director: You mean these created children have minds of their own?

Scientist: Yes, of course.

Director: Then nothing with a mind of its own should be known? We shouldn't know our friends, our neighbors?

Scientist: No, of course we should. Just not with the knowledge of making.

Director: But I thought making is how we really know.

Scientist: Well, it is.

Director: Then why would we ever be satisfied with anything but that?

Scientist: We have to be satisfied with what's possible. Are we really going to say we can make our friends?

Director: Humor me a bit. What if our friends were made in a lab and kept in that lab under strict control? Would it be possible to know them with the knowledge of making?

Scientist: If we really knew what we were doing and kept on working to shape them, to make them into what we want? Yes, I suppose it would be possible. But it would take an unbelievably extensive and highly controlled lab.

Director: Exactly how extensive and controlled?

Scientist: Ideally? The lab would have to be as extensive as the whole outside world.

Director: So we'd simply have to make the world our lab?

Scientist: Yes.

Director: And what about control?

Scientist: We'd need total control.

Director: You're talking about an absolute tyranny of science?

Scientist: Yes. That's what it would take to know people the way you're saying you want to know them.

Director: But tell me, Scientist. Tyrants don't have true friends, do they?

Scientist: Not the last time I checked.

Director: So what would be the point of having complete knowledge of my friends, if they aren't really my friends?

Scientist: There would be no point.

Director: Well, I'm finding it hard to believe.

Scientist: What?

Director: That a scientist would ever say there's no point to having complete knowledge.

Scientist: There's a point to having complete knowledge of everything in the world except for one thing, Director. Human beings.

Director: That may be, Scientist. But how do we know at what point along the way to complete knowledge we should stop?

110. KNOWING 2 (ARTIST)

Director: How does an artist know when his work is good?

Artist: Well, there are two ways. He can know from his own knowledge, or he can know from the reactions of others.

Director: Which way is your way?

Artist: I like to know from my own knowledge.

Director: Why?

Artist: Because people's reactions aren't reliable.

Director: What do you mean?

Artist: I mean, suppose I get a strongly favorable reaction to one of my works. And then suppose the next day those same people who reacted well to my work react well to someone else's work, work that I think is no good.

Director: That would cheapen their favorable reaction to your work?

Artist: Yes.

Director: But what if you only care for the reaction of certain people, not people in general?

Artist: You mean people whose judgment I respect?

Director: Yes.

Artist: Then wouldn't I have even more incentive to know my work is good? I mean, would I want to put bad work before them? I'd be embarrassed to give them anything but the best.

Director: So there's no getting around knowing from your own knowledge whether your work is good?

Artist: None that I can see.

Director: Well, how do you come to know whether your work is any good?

Artist: I'm not sure exactly. With certain works I just know it somehow.

Director: And you're satisfied with just knowing it somehow?

Artist: Well, I'd rather know how I know it.

Director: Then let's look at it this way and maybe we'll see. Do you want your work to have an effect on people?

Artist: Of course I do.

Director: Do you know what kind of effect you want or do you just hope for any sort of effect?

Artist: No, I know what kind of effect I want.

Director: If you produce a work and then show it to people, can you know what effect it has on them?

Artist: Yes, to some extent.

Director: And if you keep on showing works to people, won't you, over time, start to get an idea about what in your work causes what effect in the audience?

Artist: I suppose. But even if you have lots of experience in producing effects, you can never really know in advance what sort of effect a given work will have.

Director: But if it produces the desired effect, that's good?

Artist: Yes, of course.

Director: And if it doesn't produce the desired effect, that's bad?

Artist: Well, not necessarily.

Director: Why not?

Artist: Because what if my work lives up to my own standards of what's good even though it fails to produce the desired effect?

Director: If it lives up to your own standards, would we say the work has integrity?

Artist: Yes. Can something that has integrity be bad, no matter the reception it gets?

Director: What happens if we answer yes to that question?

Artist: We cut the only anchor that an artist has.

111. Knowing 3 (Friend)

Friend: He didn't have to say anything. He shot me a knowing glance.

Director: What exactly does that phrase mean?

Friend: You don't know?

Director: I thought I did. But now I'm not so sure.

Friend: Well, it just means that the way he looked at me told me that he knew.

Director: But what if he just happened to be looking at you?

Friend: It's not the mere fact that he looked at me. It's how he looked at me.

Director: How did he look at you?

Friend: He held my gaze for a moment.

Director: So any time I hold someone's gaze, I'm telling him that I know?

Friend: No. The context is important.

Director: So any time I hold someone's gaze when the context is right, I'm telling him that I know?

Friend: Yes.

Director: What makes the context right?

Friend: I'm not sure how to explain it.

Director: How about this for a context? I'm telling a lie and someone holds my gaze for a moment. Is it a knowing glance?

Friend: Not necessarily. The person might be trying to show that he believes you.

Director: What about this for a context? I'm describing a painful experience and someone holds my gaze for a moment. A knowing glance?

Friend: Well, it could just be sympathy, not knowledge.

Director: Then what makes a knowing glance a knowing glance?

Friend: It's more than just the glance. It's the facial expression that goes along with it.

Director: So what facial expression does it take? A smile? A frown?

Friend: No, it's not necessarily either of those.

Director: Let me guess. It depends on the context.

Friend: Yes, it does.

Director: Well, Friend, I don't feel any closer to knowing what a knowing glance is. But I have a question. Does a knowing glance necessarily involve knowledge?

Friend: What do you mean?

Director: I mean, can someone shoot a knowing glance without actually knowing?

Friend: I suppose that's possible.

Director: What makes it possible?

Friend: He thinks he knows.

Director: And when we think we know, we either know or we don't?

Friend: Yes.

Director: What do we do with those who think they know?

Friend: I'm not sure I understand what you're asking.

Director: Don't we have to find out whether they actually know what they think they know?

Friend: Yes, I suppose we do.

Director: How do we do that?

Friend: I guess we have to speak with them.

Director: Ah.

Friend: What?

Director: That's what a knowing glance is.

Friend: What is it?

Director: Why, it's nothing more, but nothing less, than an invitation — an invitation to talk.

112. DIALOGUE (FRIEND)

Director: What's the point of dialogue?

Friend: The point? You don't think dialogue is good for its own sake?

Director: No, I don't. We can go on talking endlessly to no purpose, can't we?

Friend: Yes, I suppose that's true. Well, what if we say that dialogue is for the sake of understanding?

Director: Can you say more?

Friend: What more is there to say?

Director: You think understanding is good for its own sake?

Friend: Don't you?

Director: I'm not sure. What does it mean to understand someone?

Friend: To be able to see things from his own point of view.

Director: And dialogue allows you to do that?

Friend: More so than any other means I'm aware of.

Director: But why would you want to see from someone else's point of view?

Friend: Because doing so can bring harmony.

Director: And harmony is always good?

Friend: You don't think we should always strive for harmony?

Director: I don't know, Friend. I mean, is it good to bring yourself into harmony with terrible criminals?

Friend: Of course not.

Director: Then it seems harmony isn't always good.

Friend: No, I guess it isn't.

Director: Now, if the reason why we want to see from someone else's point of view, the reason why we want to understand the person, is to bring harmony, and the harmony isn't good, do we really want to see from this person's point of view?

Friend: But if we don't see from that person's point of view, how will we know that the harmony won't be good?

Director: So we want to understand in order to know whether we should strive for harmony?

Friend: Yes, I think that's true.

Director: And are we still of the view that dialogue is for the sake of understanding?

Friend: I don't see what else it could be for.

Director: So if it's not for the sake of understanding, we can say it's for no good purpose?

Friend: I agree.

Director: And if it's not for a good purpose, it's for no purpose?

Friend: I know that's what you want to say, Director. But we have to remember that it could be for a bad purpose, too.

Director: Yes, that's true. But when dialogue is for a bad purpose, whose purpose is it?

Friend: What do you mean?

Director: I mean, isn't dialogue always between two or more willing parties? Or do you think the unwilling can participate in a dialogue?

Friend: No, all parties have to be willing.

Director: And they all will the purpose?

Friend: Well, you can willingly participate in a dialogue but not will its purpose.

Director: But if one person wills one thing, and the other wills something else — what's the purpose?

Friend: I guess there's more than one purpose.

Director: So you could go through an entire dialogue without sharing a purpose with the other?

Friend: Yes, I suppose that's true. But in that case would you ever really come to understand that person?

Director: I don't see why not. After all, what reveals the truth about another more than determined resistance to his will?

113. Harmony (Artist)

Artist: Dissonance can be pleasing in any form of art.

Director: What's pleasing about it?

Artist: It's the unexpected.

Director: You mean if dissonance is the rule it's not pleasing?

Artist: Right. You have to work with the expected and then push things into the unexpected from time to time.

Director: But what if you're someone who doesn't appreciate the unexpected?

Artist: Well, I'm only telling you about my style. There are plenty of artists who steer clear of dissonance altogether, just as there are some who only work with dissonance.

Director: I see. Then I'm wondering if you can help me understand something.

Artist: I'll try.

Director: It has to do with harmonies.

Artist: What about them?

Director: Do you believe there are natural harmonies?

Artist: Do you mean harmonies that always have been and always will be?

Director: Yes.

Artist: It's hard to say. It depends on what you mean by harmony.

Director: Let's say harmony is a pleasing combination.

Artist: Alright. The answer is no, I don't think there are natural harmonies.

Director: Why not?

Artist: Because tastes change.

Director: You mean a combination that was pleasing five thousand years ago might not be pleasing today?

Artist: Yes, of course.

Director: So when you create harmonies in your work, you don't expect that they'll always be pleasing?

Artist: No, I don't.

Director: Then you have no hope of creating timeless classics?

Artist: Well, it's more complicated than that. Tastes go through cycles.

Director: So the combination that was pleasing five thousand years ago and isn't pleasing today might well be pleasing again in another five thousand years?

Artist: Yes.

Director: Hmm. Then tell me. Would it ever make sense for an artist to create nothing but harmonies that were pleasing five thousand years ago but aren't pleasing today?

Artist: I don't see what the point would be.

Director: Couldn't the point be to please those who don't share the contemporary taste, those who are waiting for things to come around full cycle again?

Artist: Assuming there are such people, then maybe. But a good artist might find a way to please their unorthodox taste by creating new harmonies, refreshing harmonies — harmonies that harmonize with but don't ape the originals.

Director: And you think that would be better?

Artist: Of course. It would be more creative.

Director: Would these new harmonies seem dissonant to those who share in the larger contemporary taste?

Artist: Yes, they would almost certainly seem dissonant.

Director: Until people get used to them? Or until people come to understand and appreciate the ancient harmonies they're meant to enhance?

Artist: Well, learning about the ancient harmonies would help people get used to these new harmonies.

Director: Yes. But now I'm wondering. Do we have available to us an infinite number of potential harmonies, so that we'll always be able to generate new ones, regardless of whether they harmonize with the ancient harmonies or not? Or is the number of harmonies limited?

Artist: I don't know, Director.

Director: Let's assume that we can run out of new harmonies, and that we have. Wouldn't it then make sense to employ the harmonies of old, the all but forgotten harmonies themselves?

Artist: If it's really true that no more new harmonies are possible? Then it seems we don't have much choice. But that might be okay. Because even though the harmonies are the same as they were in days of old, the orientation of contemporary people toward these harmonies will differ greatly from the orientation of the people of old, even among those who might be waiting for the full cycle of time. In other words, the effect of the old harmonies on contemporaries will be different than the effect they had on the original audience.

Director: But how do you know this is true?

Artist: I know this because people evolve. And this evolution means that, in the end, the effect of something old will always be something new.

114. SCIENCE 3 (SCIENTIST)

Director: Science abhors dissonance?

Scientist: Yes, of course. It wants all scientific knowledge to be neatly in harmony. Dissonance is contradiction and contradiction means we don't know.

Director: So what happens when someone proves something that's not in harmony with the rest of science?

Scientist: He's really proved it? Then the rest of science needs to take stock and figure out where the problem lies.

Director: But what if there is no problem?

Scientist: What do you mean?

Director: What if the contradiction just means that certain truths are contradictory but are nonetheless true?

Scientist: It doesn't work that way. Contradictory truths are invitations to discover greater harmonies.

Director: Even at the cost of the original truth?

Scientist: No, of course not. Harmonies have to leave the underlying truths intact.

Director: And you believe we'll always be able to find these harmonies?

Scientist: Yes. That's the faith of the scientist. That's what keeps him going as he tries to figure things out.

Director: But what if the scientist decides to hear certain things as harmonies when in fact they're not?

Scientist: Decides to hear? You either hear them or you don't, Director.

Director: And how do you know if you've heard them?

Scientist: It all gets back to contradictions. If there are no contradictions then there's harmony.

Director: But who's to say what a contradiction is?

Scientist: Anyone. Look, if I say this substance can't react with that substance, and someone else says it can, we have a contradiction, right?

Director: Of course. But what if you say this substance is beautiful and someone else says it isn't?

Scientist: Beauty isn't a matter of science.

Director: But what about elegant theories? Aren't they beautiful?

Scientist: Yes, they are. But they're beautiful because they're simple and because they don't contradict anything else.

Director: But what if a new theory contradicts an older theory? What if it says it's wrong? Can it be beautiful?

Scientist: Yes, but that's because the new theory isn't contradicting any facts. It's only contradicting another theory.

Director: So all theories are at the mercy of the facts?

Scientist: Of course.

Director: Then who's to say what a fact is?

Scientist: Facts are facts, Director.

Director: So if you say it's a fact that this substance can never come of that substance, and someone else says it's a fact that it sometimes, though rarely, can — who's to say what the fact is?

Scientist: The one who can prove the fact.

Director: You mean the one who can show us the fact is a fact with no room for doubt?

Scientist: Yes.

Director: But what if there is room for doubt? What if neither side can prove his truth to a certainty?

Scientist: Well, then we know we're operating in the realm of probable facts.

Director: And when dealing in the realm of probable facts, which facts is science likely to prefer? Those that harmonize with the dominant view or those that don't?

Scientist: The dominant view always has the advantage.

Director: Then that seems to be good reason why the greatest minds should always tend toward other views.

115. SCIENCE 4 (*FRIEND*)

Director: I've never really understood the difference between science and technology.

Friend: Isn't technology just the application of scientific knowledge for practical purposes?

Director: That's what I've been told. But doesn't that seem to imply that science isn't practical?

Friend: Yes, but aren't there many things we know through science that aren't practical?

Director: Name one.

Friend: I'm not sure I can, offhand like this.

Director: What about the location of the farthest star in the universe? Is that a matter of science?

Friend: Yes.

Director: Is it practical?

Friend: Not really.

Director: But it might one day be practical?

Friend: Yes, one day maybe.

Director: What would make it practical?

Friend: Our being able to do something with it.

Director: Like travel to that star?

Friend: Sure.

Director: And it would take technology to travel to the star?

Friend: Of course.

Director: Could we develop the technology to travel to a faraway star without knowing its location?

Friend: You're asking if technology can do without science?

Director: Yes.

Friend: Well, I suppose it could blindly grope its way toward faraway stars and get there eventually.

Director: Science is the eyes of technology?

Friend: Yes, of course.

Director: But what if science itself gropes its way toward its truths?

Friend: That wouldn't change the fact that the truths of science guide technology.

Director: No, I suppose that's true. But then wouldn't it be a case of the blind leading the blind?

Friend: But scientific truths allow us to see.

Director: So before there was science, no one could see?

Friend: Not the way we can see now.

Director: How do we know the way we see now is the right way to see?

Friend: We know because we can do things that couldn't be done before science.

Director: So the ultimate end and justification of science is doing?

Friend: Yes, I think that's true.

Director: And this means science can't reach its end or be justified without technology, without that which allows us to do?

Friend: Right.

Director: I see. But how do we know what we want to do?

Friend: How do we know? We just know.

Director: We just know with no questions asked?

Friend: No, we can question what we want.

Director: Yes, that's true. But how many of us really ever do that, Friend?

Friend: Well, not many, I suppose.

Director: Then we may be more blind than we think.

116. TASTES 1 (*SCIENTIST*)

Scientist: Tastes change.

Director: Why do they change?

Scientist: More often than not? Because we mature.

Director: Does this just hold for individuals or can the tastes of a people change?

Scientist: The tastes of a people certainly can change.

Director: And can we make a scientific study of this change?

Scientist: Yes, of course. There are several branches of science that can and do make such studies.

Director: How do these studies proceed?

Scientist: Well, the simplest way is to ask people about their tastes.

Director: You mean through surveys?

Scientist: Yes.

Director: So people just tell you what they like and what they don't like?

Scientist: Right.

Director: But what if they lie?

Scientist: That's always the problem with surveys.

Director: Why do you think someone would lie about his tastes?

Scientist: Because he's embarrassed to admit the truth.

Director: What would be embarrassing about the truth?

Scientist: Having a taste for things that are frowned upon.

Director: Who does the frowning?

Scientist: Society.

Director: Yes, but that's not the only possibility, is it? Couldn't someone be embarrassed even if society doesn't frown on the taste?

Scientist: Well, I suppose if someone in that person's life, someone important, frowns on the taste, the person might not want to own up to having it.

Director: Not even in an anonymous survey?

Scientist: In some cases I don't think the person even admits it to himself.

Director: But let's get specific. What might such a taste be? A taste for philosophy?

Scientist: Sure, it could be a taste for that. But let's use a simpler example. Let's say it could be a taste for a certain type of music.

Director: So if someone important to me despises this music, I might not admit I have a taste for it, even to myself?

Scientist: Yes.

Director: And that's so even if society as a whole has no problem allowing me to listen to it?

Scientist: Yes, that's the extreme case. You could listen to it but you don't allow yourself to.

Director: Do you think this is healthy?

Scientist: No, of course not.

Director: Would it be healthier to listen to this music in secret than not to listen to it at all?

Scientist: Well, secrecy brings its own problems. It would be better to listen to the music in the open.

Director: Even if that means a break with the important person in my life?

Scientist: If that person is willing to break with you over something as harmless as music, then there are other problems in play here.

Director: Agreed. But what do you think, Scientist? All that we've said about the individual and music, does it all apply to society as a whole?

Scientist: To society as a whole? But who could be the important person in the life of society frowning on its taste, the person it might break with?

Director: I don't know. But I think that's a good question to ask.

117. TASTES 2 (ARTIST)

Artist: No, of course my work isn't to everyone's taste.

Director: It's only to the taste of people with good taste?

Artist: Would you blame me if I said yes?

Director: No, I wouldn't blame you at all. When you make something that you present to the public, you think it's good, and those who like what's good have good taste, right?

Artist: Right.

Director: But here's the hard question. Do you think most people have good taste?

Artist: Honestly? No.

Director: So most people don't like your work? Or can people who don't have good taste like your work?

Artist: No, by definition, if you don't have good taste you don't like good work. So, no, most people don't like my work.

Director: Is that the way it is with everything?

Artist: What do you mean?

Director: I mean, if someone builds a house, he either does good work or not, right?

Artist: Of course.

Director: When it comes to living in that house, people will like it if it was made with good work?

Artist: True.

Director: And these people would have good taste? I mean, they appreciate good work and we said that only people with good taste appreciate good work, didn't we?

Artist: Yes.

Director: Will more people than not appreciate a well made house? Or is it like it is with your work, and most people won't like the well made house?

Artist: Almost everyone will like the well made house.

Director: So we're seeing something strange, aren't we? Most people will like, will have a taste for, a well made house, but most people have no taste for a well made work of art. Or isn't that the way it is?

Artist: I think we're distorting things.

Director: Oh, how?

Artist: It's not right to say that liking a well made house is a matter of taste.

Director: Why not?

Artist: Because it's a practical matter.

Director: And we don't have tastes when it comes to practical matters?

Artist: Not like we do when it comes to art.

Director: But really, Artist, you surprise me. Are you saying that art is simply impractical?

Artist: Well, it's not practical in the way a house is.

Director: But isn't it good to think of it like this? The house is the dwelling for the body while art is the dwelling for the soul?

Artist: I think it is good.

Director: And isn't a home for the soul every bit as practical as a home for the body?

Artist: I suppose that's true

Director: So how do we account for the difference in taste that we find when it comes to houses and works of art?

Artist: I think I understand it now. There is, generally speaking, just one type of body. But there are many types of soul.

Director: And you want to make art for the rare type of soul?

Artist: Yes.

Director: But how do you know what sort of dwelling suits it best?

Artist: I know because I've been studying that type of soul all my life.

Director: And let me guess — that type of soul is yours.

118. Tastes 3 (Friend)

Director: Friend, do you believe it's possible to educate your taste?

Friend: You mean can you learn to appreciate something?

Director: Yes.

Friend: That's definitely possible.

Director: What do you think is a good example of the phenomenon?

Friend: Learning to appreciate fine wine.

Director: Can't you just taste fine wine and enjoy it, no education involved?

Friend: Sure, but you enjoy it more when you know more about it.

Director: So I'll like a wine more if I know something about the region it's from?

Friend: Well, not that alone.

Director: What else do I need to know?

Friend: You need to be able to describe the wine.

Director: So I can tell you all about it?

Friend: No, that's not the point. I'm talking about being able to describe it to yourself.

Director: I can't fully appreciate it if I can't describe it to myself?

Friend: Not fully.

Director: But doesn't it taste the same, regardless of whether I describe it to myself as I'm tasting it or not?

Friend: I'm not so sure it does.

Director: Why not?

Friend: Because you might not notice the subtleties.

Director: You mean I might miss a note of this, a hint of that?

Friend: Yes, exactly.

Director: And my education consists in learning to notice and describe these subtleties?

Friend: Right.

Director: Do you think it's only like that with wine?

Friend: No, it can be like that with anything that involves subtleties.

Director: That makes me wonder. Can an expert in the subtleties of wine teach me to appreciate the subtleties in a work of art?

Friend: Not strictly speaking as a wine expert, no.

Director: I'd need to find an expert in works of art?

Friend: You'd need to find an expert in the particular type of art you want to appreciate.

Director: So it's not enough to find a generalist in all types of fine art if I want to learn to fully appreciate Renaissance portraiture in particular?

Friend: Not if the generalist isn't an expert in that type of portraiture.

Director: I see. But what happens if I want to learn to appreciate something new and strange, something that has yet to have experts?

Friend: It's not easy to learn in that case.

Director: Agreed. But how would I go about it?

Friend: You'd have to educate yourself.

Director: You mean I'd have to make a study of the thing?

Friend: Yes. But you'd have to be willing to put in a lot of time and effort, Director.

Director: Suppose I'm willing. Suppose I'm so taken by the thing I can't help myself. What will happen?

Friend: You might become the first expert.

Director: You mean I might be the one who first teaches others how to appreciate it?

Friend: Yes.

Director: Then it seems I'd better know the thing, in all its subtlety, very, very well.

119. PRIDE 1 (SCIENTIST)

Director: What do you take most pride in, Scientist? Is it your contribution to mankind's body of knowledge?

Scientist: No, actually. I take pride in my mind.

Director: Your mind? Do you mean your ability to process information?

Scientist: No, not that.

Director: Do you mean your memory?

Scientist: No, not that either.

Director: Then what is it about your mind that you take pride in?

Scientist: I'm proud of my intellectual honesty.

Director: How is that different than simple honesty? I mean, why not just say you're proud of your honesty?

Scientist: It's a matter of emphasis, Director. Intellectual honesty calls attention to the temptations of those who work with their minds.

Director: But don't we all, to some degree, work with our minds?

Scientist: Yes, but it's really a question of degree here.

Director: And the work you do is eminently work of the mind?

Scientist: Yes.

Director: Would you say no one works with the mind more than a scientist?

Scientist: I would.

Director: What about a lab technician? Does he work with the mind?

Scientist: Yes, but not as much as the scientist who runs the lab.

Director: What specifically is the difference between the two?

Scientist: The scientist understands why things are being done the way they are in the lab, more so than the tech does.

Director: So understanding why is the work of the mind?

Scientist: Understanding why comes from the work of the mind.

Director: Then a great understanding implies that great work of the mind has been done?

Scientist: Yes.

Director: So where does honesty come in?

Scientist: It comes in the connection between the work and the understanding.

Director: You mean if I perform work in my mind, intellectual honesty requires me to come to an understanding that squares with the work I've performed?

Scientist: Precisely. Sometimes a man of science will perform work that suggests one thing but he allows himself to understand, to believe, something else.

Director: This must have to do with the temptations you mentioned.

Scientist: Yes, of course. People who work with their minds are often tempted to believe what they want to believe and not what their work indicates is true.

Director: So that's intellectual honesty? Believing what you know is true?

Scientist: Yes. Can you see why I'd be most proud of that?

Director: I can, Scientist. But then there's just one thing I think we need to clear up.

Scientist: By all means. What?

Director: Can't you believe what you know is true but then speak falsely about it to others?

Scientist: Yes, I suppose you can. But why would you ever want to do that?

Director: It's hard to say. But would you maintain your intellectual honesty if you did?

Scientist: Well, according to what we've said, yes. But then that has to mean that intellectual honesty alone isn't enough.

Director: Yes, but it makes for an excellent start.

120. PRIDE 2 (ARTIST)

Director: Artist, are you proud of your work?

Artist: Sometimes.

Director: When are you proud? When you come up with a good idea?

Artist: Well, good ideas are important. But I wouldn't be proud just because I came up with a good idea.

Director: Why not?

Artist: Because you have to execute on that good idea.

Director: And execution is the hard part?

Artist: It is.

Director: How do you know when you've executed well?

Artist: You know when your execution makes the good idea better.

Director: What exactly makes the idea better?

Artist: Employing means that make the idea more interesting than it otherwise would have been.

Director: Does that work with bad ideas?

Artist: Why would you want to make a bad idea more interesting?

Director: Maybe you lack good ideas. Would you be proud to make a bad idea better?

Artist: No, of course not. I'm only proud when I make good ideas better.

Director: What makes an idea good?

Artist: It tells the truth about the world.

Director: So your art makes the truth better? Makes it more interesting?

Artist: Yes, it presents the truth in a way that makes you want more of it.

Director: You mean your work, when it's good, creates an appetite for truth?

Artist: Yes.

Director: So you're a sort of chef?

Artist: Sure.

Director: Then you're proud when people eat the whole meal and ask for more?

Artist: What chef wouldn't be?

Director: But do you make gluttons of people?

Artist: Can you really have too much truth?

Director: So you keep on cooking and they keep on eating? And the higher quality the food, the more they'll want?

Artist: That's how it goes.

Director: But you know what the problem is, don't you?

Artist: Certainly. Not every food is to everyone's taste.

Director: Do you believe different truths appeal to different people?

Artist: I do.

Director: So how do you decide what sort of meal to prepare?

Artist: I create dishes that I would want to eat.

Director: Then if you like the flavor of what you put together, you're proud?

Artist: Yes.

Director: Are you even more proud if others also like the taste?

Artist: Naturally.

Director: But you're still proud even if you're all alone in the truth?

Artist: Well, yes, because if it tastes good, it is good. And I should be proud of creating something that's good.

Director: Then dare to create those things that, as far as you're aware, you're the only one who likes. And never forget that certain tastes are acquired tastes, and acquiring a taste takes time. But when the time eventually comes, Artist, I think you'll find others, others who will appreciate your truths, who will wish to sit down with you at your table.

121. PRIDE 3 (*FRIEND*)

Friend: Director, what are you proud of?

Director: I'm proud of my friends.

Friend: No, really. What are you proud of?

Director: I'm serious, Friend.

Friend: So you're proud of me?

Director: Yes, of course.

Friend: Why would you be proud of me?

Director: Because you have qualities I admire.

Friend: Name one.

Director: I admire the fact that you're challenging me right now.

Friend: But most people get upset when they're challenged.

Director: You and I aren't most people. And that's another thing I admire about you.

Friend: That I'm not most people? Then what am I?

Director: You're Friend.

Friend: Just as you're Director?

Director: What else?

Friend: But you have reason to be proud. I don't.

Director: What reason do you think I have?

Friend: You know things.

Director: What things?

Friend: Things in general.

Director: You and I have been friends for almost longer than I can remember, and you can't say what I know more than that?

Friend: Then you tell me what you know.

Director: I know it's good to be proud.

Friend: Yes, but you also know it's only good to be proud when you have reason to be proud.

Director: Yes, that's true. But don't you and I share a reason? Aren't you proud of your friends?

Friend: Well, I'm proud of having you as a friend.

Director: What about your other friends?

Friend: I'm not so proud of them.

Director: Why not?

Friend: You know, I've never thought about it in so many words before. But I think it's because they get upset when they're challenged.

Director: Why do you think they get upset?

Friend: Because they're too proud.

Director: Now isn't that ironic? So are you suggesting there's only so much pride that's good for a person?

Friend: I am.

Director: And how do you know how much is enough?

Friend: I don't know how much is enough. But I know too much when I see it.

Director: Well, that's fortunate, Friend — because I know too little when I see it. So why don't we make a point of encouraging one another to find the amount of pride that's right? I can't think of any more important work among friends.

122. DEATH (*SCIENTIST*)

Scientist: Yes, I'm afraid of death.

Director: Why?

Scientist: Because I don't know what happens when we die.

Director: But you're a scientist.

Scientist: Scientists can be afraid of death.

Director: But I thought scientists love to confront the unknown.

Scientist: So you think we should see death as some sort of final frontier?

Director: Why not?

Scientist: Well, I'll try to think of it that way.

Director: But wouldn't knowledge of death and what, if anything, lies beyond be among the greatest of prizes that science could claim?

Scientist: I have to agree.

Director: And yet you're still more afraid than excited?

Scientist: I'd rather solve the mysteries of death from this side of the grave.

Director: Do you believe in ghosts?

Scientist: What? No, of course not.

Director: Why not?

Scientist: Because there's no convincing scientific proof of their existence.

Director: And yet many people believe in ghosts.

Scientist: Many people used to believe in witches, too.

Director: But these people swear they've had encounters with ghosts. And they're not exactly few in number.

Scientist: Yes, but how many scientists have had encounters with ghosts? Not so many.

Director: Maybe scientists are disposed in such a way that ghosts leave them alone.

Scientist: Are you being serious?

Director: Well, isn't that possible?

Scientist: Of course it's possible. But it's also ridiculous.

Director: Why?

Scientist: Because you can make that claim about any crazy belief that people might have. The sane people don't experience the crazy because the crazy avoids the sane.

Director: But doesn't it make perfectly good sense to say that what you're calling the crazy, if given the choice, would avoid what you're calling the sane?

Scientist: Crazy sticks to crazy as sane sticks to sane? Now you're making me wonder about your sanity, Director.

Director: I've never seen a ghost, if that's what you're asking.

Scientist: Then why take the side of those who claim to experience these things?

Director: Oh, I'm not taking their side. I'm just trying to make sense of things.

Scientist: But if you try to make sense of something that's essentially senseless, what are you really doing?

Director: But here again, Scientist, I must have recourse to the fundamental claim of science.

Scientist: What do you mean?

Director: Isn't it the goal of science to make sense of what seems to be senseless?

Scientist: Well, that's true. But science can't waste its time on this sort of thing.

Director: Is it a waste of time to prove to those who believe in ghosts that ghosts don't exist, if you can really prove they don't?

Scientist: But that's the thing. It's almost impossible to prove that something doesn't exist. And, beyond that, I have no doubt whatsoever that it's completely impossible to stay ahead of whatever crazy new beliefs people might conjure up.

Director: Then that's good news, right? There will always be work for science.

123. Satisfaction 1 (Friend)

Friend: Director, what satisfies you most?

Director: Most? Of all the things in my life?

Friend: Yes.

Director: But let me make sure what you're asking is clear. Do you believe satisfaction is the highest feeling obtainable by man?

Friend: Yes, I do. But I also believe satisfaction is the deepest feeling obtainable by man.

Director: So satisfaction is the complete feeling, the feeling that sweeps from the lowest to the highest in us?

Friend: Yes, I think that puts it well.

Director: And to the extent that the good is something we feel, the greatest good we can achieve is satisfaction?

Friend: Yes.

Director: And the greatest good is the most important thing in life?

Friend: It is.

Director: So you're basically asking me what is the most important thing in my life?

Friend: I am.

Director: What if I tell you it's friendship?

Friend: I'd say I think that's great.

Director: And what if I tell you it's knowledge?

Friend: That, too, would be great.

Director: And what about understanding?

Friend: Are you saying all three of them are equally important to you?

Director: Hold on a minute. There's more. What if I tell you the most import thing in my life is wealth, or power, or fame?

Friend: I wouldn't believe you.

Director: What if I tell you it's vindication, justice, or victory?

Friend: Then I wouldn't be sure whether to believe you or not. But, Director, just tell me what the most important thing in your life is.

Director: Will you be satisfied if I tell you what the thing is that allows me to choose from among these things?

Friend: What is it?

Director: Philosophy, the true helpmate of choice.

Friend: Of course. I should have known you'd say that. But then what does philosophy say is most important?

Director: Well, now I'm almost embarrassed to say.

Friend: Why?

Director: Because one time it says this is most important, and another time it says that.

Friend: Philosophy tells you at times that wealth, or power, or fame is most important?

Director: Yes. At times I need to concentrate on each of these things. I need money to live. I need power in order to accomplish things at work. And I need a little fame, a bit of solid repute, to sustain me from time to time.

Friend: But just because you need those things that doesn't mean they're what's most important in life.

Director: Tell me, Friend. What's most important to a pyramid — bottom, middle, or top?

Friend: They're equally important, assuming you want a complete pyramid.

Director: So when someone is building his pyramid in life, doesn't whatever part he's working on seem most important at the time?

Friend: Yes, but you can't jeopardize one part for the sake of another.

Director: Of course not.

Friend: And you can't get around choosing which part goes on top.

124. SATISFACTION 2 (ARTIST)

Artist: That's what satisfies me concerning my own work. But now you want to know what satisfies me concerning the work of others?

Director: Yes. Do you hold others to the same standard you hold yourself?

Artist: No, not necessarily.

Director: Do you hold them to a higher standard?

Artist: No, I generally hold them to a lower standard.

Director: Why would you do that? Why be harder on yourself than you are on others, Artist?

Artist: I know. It doesn't make sense, does it?

Director: Do you think your work is better than that of others because of the higher standard?

Artist: Honestly? I don't know if it is or not.

Director: Hmm. Do you ever go back and revisit your work long after you've finished it?

Artist: Sometimes.

Director: When you do, does it feel familiar or does it feel strange?

Artist: That's a funny question. But I know exactly what you mean. At first it feels strange. But then when I warm to it, it feels familiar.

Director: And once it feels familiar, if you were satisfied before, you're satisfied again?

Artist: Yes.

Director: And when you take in the work of others, does it feel familiar or strange?

Artist: It's the same sort of thing. At first it almost always feels strange, but if I warm to it, it feels familiar.

Director: And you can't be satisfied unless the work feels familiar to you?

Artist: No, I can't.

Director: Could that be your low standard for others? That their work feel familiar? Or does it take something more?

Artist: I'm not sure feeling familiar is such a low standard.

Director: Then maybe you'd consider applying that same standard to yourself? Tell me. Do you think it's possible for you to create something that doesn't feel familiar to you when you return to it, not even after you've tried to warm to it?

Artist: I'm afraid this is going to sound crazy, but I do.

Director: And how is that possible?

Artist: Maybe I've changed.

Director: But even if you've changed, don't you think what you were will always, in a way, be part of you?

Artist: Yes, I do.

Director: So you'll always, eventually, be able to warm to what you created?

Artist: I'm not sure, Director. I mean, suppose I create something at a time when I don't know myself, truly know myself. Then suppose I come to know myself. Will I really warm to what I made when I didn't know myself? Do you see what I'm saying?

Director: Yes, I think I see. What you made will seem strange to you.

Artist: Yes.

Director: So what does that mean for others?

Artist: What do you mean?

Director: Might there be someone who finds what you made when you didn't know yourself to be familiar?

Artist: I suppose that's possible.

Director: And it might satisfy him?

Artist: Yes, it might.

Director: What would you say to him if he approached you?

Artist: What could I say? I'd have no choice but to show him the way.

Director: The way?

Artist: To where I am now.

125. BEGINNINGS 4 (FRIEND)

Director: Friend, does a good ending necessarily follow from a good beginning?

Friend: No, of course not.

Director: What does it take to connect a good beginning to a good ending?

Friend: Many good steps along the way.

Director: What does it take to connect a bad beginning to a good ending?

Friend: The same.

Director: So with many good steps we can dispose of the need for a good beginning?

Friend: Well, in a sense. But a good beginning points you to the first good step.

Director: And a bad beginning points you to a bad first step?

Friend: Yes. And step follows step.

Director: So if you had a bad beginning, how do you ever point yourself to a good step?

Friend: It's very hard, Director.

Director: Does it involve learning that your beginning was bad?

Friend: Yes, I think it does.

Director: And if those with bad beginnings must learn that their beginnings were bad, don't those with good beginnings have to learn that their beginnings were good?

Friend: That's true. It's not always obvious how good or bad things were until later.

Director: So by the time you figure out whether your beginning was good or bad, you must have already taken many steps, no?

Friend: Yes.

Director: But as you take step after step, doesn't the importance of the beginning diminish?

Friend: It does. The steps themselves count most.

Director: So if you can only learn what steps are good, your beginning doesn't matter?

Friend: I wouldn't say that.

Director: Why not?

Friend: Because your beginning influences you, to some extent, your whole life.

Director: So if I had a good beginning, I'll always be at least somewhat inclined to take good steps? And if I had a bad beginning, I'll always be somewhat inclined toward bad?

Friend: Don't you think that's how it goes?

Director: I'm not sure. That would mean that one type of person has to learn to go with his inclinations, and another type has to learn to go against them. Wouldn't it?

Friend: I'm afraid that's true.

Director: But would that be fair?

Friend: Of course it wouldn't be fair. Life isn't fair.

Director: But what happens if you change your mind?

Friend: What do you mean?

Director: What if you think you had a bad beginning but later decide it was good?

Friend: Good how?

Director: Good in that it prepared you for life. For being strong. For being independent. Things like that.

Friend: Then the beginning would have indeed been good.

Director: But what if despite that beginning you find yourself heading toward a bad end?

Friend: There's only one thing to do. Take a step toward the good. And then another.

Director: But how do you know what's good if you've long been on a bad way?

Friend: If you know the way is bad, that means you must have some idea of which way is good.

Director: And if you switch ways, and stick to the new way, what have you done?

Friend: You've given yourself that rarest of opportunities — a chance at the closest thing possible to a fresh new start.

Printed in the United States
By Bookmasters